Saintly Women

OF MODERN TIMES

"We need to cultivate, think upon, and seek the companionship of those saints who, though living on earth like ourselves, have accomplished such great deeds for God."

ST. TERESA OF ÁVILA

Saintly Women

OF MODERN TIMES

Joan Carroll Cruz

TAN Books
Charlotte, North Carolina

Table of Contents

Acknowledgments

⌘

$\mathcal{H}$ow can one adequately show appreciation for the kindness
and generosity of so many who answered my queries about
the holy people mentioned in the present volume? The interest
in these works by so many is truly a humbling experience. Those
who answered my queries and sent books, booklets pamphlets, pic-
tures, and various documents include archbishops, bishops, postulators and vice postulators, numerous organizations, relatives of the
subjects mentioned, and various individuals. Had it not been for
the help of these good people, it would have been impossible to
portray adequately these saintly individuals, since many of these
20th-century people are not well-known, having only lately been
designated as Servants of God.

Since one or two names inadvertently might be missed, were
I to list the names of all who helped me, I am asking their forgiveness in not mentioning them by name. I am, however, deeply
grateful for their gracious assistance, which has been an inspiration
to me. I extend to all of them my deepest appreciation and respect.
I pray that the good Lord will abundantly bless their kindness, and
that the saintly people mentioned in the three volumes will look
kindly upon them. To all I extend my profound respect and deepest
appreciation.

Foreword

❧

The Catholic Church has been graced with a bountiful array of saints, but, as we know, the greater majority are nuns and priests. By comparison, we have only a small fraction of lay men and women who were declared by the Church as having merited the honors of the altar. Since we are encouraged to imitate the virtues of the saints, wouldn't it seem more appropriate if we had models of holiness who lived outside the cloister in the secular world—saints who endured the struggles and difficulties of everyday life as we encounter in secular surroundings? As St. Teresa of Ávila has written, "We need to cultivate and think upon, and seek the companionship of those saints who, though living on earth like ourselves, have accomplished such great deeds for God."

In my book *Secular Saints*, examples were given of almost two hundred fifty lay men and women who, if not already canonized, were on their way to canonization. They came from the early days of the Church, through the ages, to the present day. In this volume, we have only twentieth-century saints, many of whom drove cars and used telephones. Some even had televisions as well as many other modern conveniences. All lived and died in the last century, with the exception of Pauline Jaricot.

It is hoped that the reader will examine the indexes that give the occupations and the difficulties of life and health that were encountered by these holy women. By making use of the indexes, readers can find a saint to whom they can relate—saints who had a similar occupation, or those who experienced the same difficulties or illnesses as readers might now be enduring.

We have here many biographies of laywomen representing many countries. They are from such diverse occupations as a rag collector, a hair dresser, and an embroidery teacher, among many other professions.

An explanation about the various titles follows.

The sole purpose in writing this book was to demonstrate, to people in every walk of life, the virtues practiced, and the cares and sufferings endured by laywomen who are now on their way to canonization. Those who have difficulties, and those who are suffering, have examples here of holy people who have had the same struggles and difficulties. It was because of these hardships, endured with prayer and confidence in God, that they attained holiness.

How did they do it? Here, then, are their secrets.

—JOAN CARROLL CRUZ

Servant of God: After five years have elapsed since death, and after the bishop of the diocese officially opens the cause of beatification, the candidate may be called a Servant of God.

Venerable: After the Congregation for the Causes of Saints receives the case, examines it and determines that it has merit, and after a number of preliminary steps have been taken, a *Decree super Virtutibus* is issued, which gives the Servant of God the title of Venerable.

Blessed: Once a miracle, worked through the intercession of the Venerable, has been canonically investigated and approved, this, together with the Decree of Heroic Virtues, is passed to the Holy Father, who decides on beatification. After the ceremony of beatification has been held, the Venerable is now given the title of Blessed.

Saint: For canonization, another miracle performed *after* the beatification ceremony is required. After the miracle has been canonically investigated and approved, the pope may perform a canonization ceremony, after which the Blessed is now given the title of Saint.

NOTE: Those without a title are holy persons whose cases are still on the diocesan level, but whose causes are expected to be officially opened in the near future.

Servant of God Adele Bonolis

1909–1980

Founder of Homes for Unfortunates

ITALY

*I*t was evident to those who knew Adele Bonolis that she was imbued with the love of God. This love enabled her to transmit serenity and peace to those who came into contact with her, especially to those she helped in the foundations she organized for the care and education of unfortunates.

She was born in Milan, Italy, to a hardworking family on August 14, 1909, one of six children. She was educated in Catholic schools and was active in the women's division of Catholic Action in the parish of St. Ambrogio. The aim of Catholic Action was to foster an intense spiritual life in its members, which in turn would inspire them to participate in charitable and apostolic work. Eventually, she assumed the responsibility for the group.

She never married, but was busy with the needs and lives of her siblings. According to Adele's good friend, Lina Saltafossi, when

Adele's mother became ill, Adele attended her and lovingly saw to her needs each day before Adele had to report for work. Staying close to her mother during that time, Adele began her ministry to the young by often instructing them from the front of her home. This continued until her mother's death in 1935.

Early in her life, Adele abandoned herself completely to the will of God and developed a rich interior life based on the Eucharist and daily sacrifices. Throughout her lifetime, she would suffer from pleurisy and other illnesses, but nothing, it is said, would prohibit her from her daily Mass, not even when she was feeling ill and had a high fever.

After receiving her commercial license, Adele worked for three successive firms. Later she enrolled in the Catholic University in Milan, from which she graduated with a degree in philosophy on November 24, 1944. These were war years with devastation and misery, which she experienced most severely when her home was totally destroyed in the bombardment.

We find her next in Sondrio and Lecco with another friend, Giuseppina Achilli. Instead of teaching philosophy, which was a more lucrative position, Adele abandoned this field in favor of directing and teaching religion to high school students. Many years later, her students remembered and admired her for the care she took in forming their consciences and instilling in them a love of their faith.

But Adele's time was not restricted to teaching. Her spare time was devoted to her activities with Catholic Action. Her talents and abilities were soon recognized when she was named to the diocesan council.

Adele was content with teaching and her work with Catholic Action. Yet she felt an overwhelming need not only to teach the young, but also to help the sick. For that reason she enrolled in the school of medicine in 1946.

However, she was not destined to graduate; God had other plans for her. Her need to help the poor and unfortunate was soon to be realized. The opportunity came in the form of a request from a judge of the court of Lecco.

He asked if she would help boys who had appeared in his court. So she directed a summer colony for them, which was so successful that she was asked to continue the experiment. Thus was founded the *Castel Vezio*, or the *Casa dei Ragazzi*, for the education and care of troublesome boys.

Together with two of her good friends and fellow workers in Catholic Action, Giovanna Negrini and Giuseppina Achilli, Adele founded the *Casa Maria Assunta*, or the House of Feminine Orientation. It opened to receive prostitutes, their children and those women being released from prisons. Here was a home for these women where they could physically and morally recover.

This was the beginning of a series of houses for the help and care of unfortunates. In 1962, Adele founded Villa Salus and the *As. Fra. Case Iris* for the mentally ill. Among the other institutions is the *Casa San Paolo*, founded in 1970, which was financially assisted by Cardinal Giovanni Montini, the future Pope Paul VI. This was established for those men discharged from jail and from the judicial insane asylums.

Another is the *Casa Maria Delle Grazie*, founded in 1972 for the education and rehabilitation of disadvantaged men and those suffering from psychiatric, physical, social, and economic problems, as well as those released from prisons. All of these substantial buildings are two to four stories high and are large, neat, and attractive. All are in active service today, staffed by qualified doctors, nurses, and social workers.

Based on what she called the "three pillars," *previdenza, prudenza,* and *provvidenza* (foresight, prudence, and providence), she worked hard not only to establish these houses, but to find the means to support her guests, to provide them with all that was necessary for their care, and to provide qualified workers. This, of course, was a difficult task with many disappointments, but her inner strength and the "three pillars," plus her love of God, sustained her.

Adele also founded an association now called the Foundation, which gathers people who desire to advance in the spiritual life. This, too, is active today.

With all her many activities and responsibilities, testimony reveals that "Adele consumed all of her existence doing good without a desire of reward or applause. . . . She gave her time and attention to the great and the humble, to the young and the elderly, listening to all with patience and love."

Her work was soon to end. Around the year 1976, Adele experience the first symptoms of an intestinal tumor and underwent an operation at the *Clinic S. Giuseppe*. The condition did not improve, but continued to advance and cause discomfort for the next four years. During this prolonged illness, she and her sister-friend Giuseppina continued to visit the various institutions, encouraging the managers and workers, and offering consolation to the residents.

Adele died on August 11, 1980, in Milan, with a reputation of great holiness. During the funeral homily by Monsignor Libero Tresoldi in *S. Ambrogio* church, he declared that Adele "was a woman of faith who had surrendered herself to God, was docile to His wishes, and had a deep capacity for greatness." She was buried in the Resurrection Cemetery of Lucinasco, Italy.

In her honor, a book was published in 1986, which included glowing testimonials attesting to her gift for charity, her love of the unfortunates, and her love of God.

Her cause for beatification has been opened, much to the satisfaction of those who knew her, and to those who were charitably helped in her many institutions. †

Amata Cerretelli

1907–1963

Founder and Carmelite Tertiary

ITALY

*A*mata Cerretelli was sickly from the day of her birth, suffering during her lifetime of fifty-six years from a variety of illnesses. So one can only marvel at her patience and pleasant humor in spite of pain that she accepted for the love of God. Yet, despite a catalog of ailments, Amata established an organization, *La Famiglia*, that is very much in operation today.

After her birth in Campi Besenzio, a village outside Florence, Italy, Amata was baptized on the day of her birth because of her frail condition. For the next nine years, she suffered from what the doctor diagnosed as rheumatism of the arteries. During brief respites, Amata could walk, but with great difficulty. This endured until she was eighteen years old, but then she developed a speech defect, and because of her illness, she was forced to walk in a stooped condition.

A family who knew her mother suggested that Amata be sent to them in the country, where she might benefit from a change of climate. But the local specialist despaired of being able to help her and suggested that she be sent home. This produced another problem, since she injured her head when she fell at the train station.

During times when she recovered a little, she helped in the family's cafe and resumed her daily attendance at Mass. Although the family experienced financial difficulties and had to sell half their property, they were able to give Amata a small allowance, which she in turn gave to the poor.

Amata's condition became critical when she was eighteen and was confined to bed for six months. The parents borrowed money to have a specialist examine their daughter, but he diagnosed her condition as grim, and he fully expected Amata to die. But to the amazement of the specialist, and the pastor who was called to administer the Sacrament of the Anointing of the Sick, Amata slowly recovered.

Then came a family crisis, when the father was arrested and falsely accused of selling black-market tobacco products. For eleven months, the father was detained in a cell with eleven other prisoners, losing weight because of the meager rations. Amata and her mother denied themselves to bring him more food, but he refused to eat what they brought, since his cellmates were also suffering privations.

Since the families of the other prisoners were far away, Amata and her mother somehow were able to bring all of them something to eat each day, even though the two women were forced to observe a strict fast. When the father was released, his license to sell tobacco was revoked, which put a heavier strain on the family business that was already experiencing a loss of trade. Unfortunately, another loan had to be made to cover medical and business expenses.

Amata's health again declined. The diagnosis was infected tonsils. An operation was performed for their removal, but because of her frail condition, she was forced to undergo the procedure without anesthesia. When she did not improve, and was experiencing excruciating pain, the doctor amended his diagnosis to include her kidneys and trouble with her spine.

After recovering, Amata was again bedridden, this time with a tumor on the bottom of her foot. Because of the family's financial situation, the doctor decided to remove the tumor in his office. The tumor, however, returned.

Fearing a malignancy, the doctor thought it best to remove the entire foot, but the mother appealed to St. Anthony with a favorable result, since the tumor disappeared. Soon after, Amata developed problems of the throat, which required a second operation. As a result, Amata was to experience slurred speech until her death.

The family was faced with more problems when they experienced difficulty in paying the interest on three loans they had made to cover expenses. A public auction was declared and their property sold. The family was given one month to vacate their home. In spite of her poor health and serious financial difficulties, Amata urged her parents to accept the will of God, with all three praying fervently that God would look after them.

With a slight improvement in her health, Amata and her friend Carmen Arini, who was to write Amata's first biography, looked for an apartment that would serve their families. When all was settled, Amata found work in a factory, where speed was expected. Because of a lack of proper nourishment and her frail health, Amata collapsed and was bedridden throughout the winter. In the spring, her father, who was also experiencing poor health, died.

Since Amata was an attractive young lady and had a number of admirers, her friends urged her to marry, since both she and her mother would then experience security. But Amata would not listen to their reasonings, declaring that this would be an unfair burden to place on a husband. Moreover, her frail condition would limit the attention she would be able to give a family.

The religious life was suggested. But again, Amata would not hear of it, saying that her vocation was to the secular state, where

God wanted her to be. Her only wish was to fulfill the duties of her state of life.

Amata next found work in a shop that manufactured artificial flowers and decorative feathers. For two years she continued at this position, even though she was afflicted with a variety of illnesses.

First, two abscesses developed around her nose that caused a swelling of her whole head and an inability to eat or drink. When a high fever developed, she was confined to bed.

Once this was cured, she developed a sciatica attack in her left thigh that lasted for a time, and even prevented her from attending Christmas Mass. When this subsided, a pain in the finger of her left hand caused such pain that a doctor recognized an infection under the nail and removed it, again without an anesthetic. A second nail was also removed.

Next, her appendix was removed, as was a large quantity of infected material from her abdomen. Her recovery lasted a month.

Amata's prayerful attitude during these trials was astounding. She accepted her pains as her participation in Our Lord's way of the Cross and as God's will for her. She endured all as her participation in Christ's passion for the redemption of the world.

The onslaught of World War II brought other difficulties when a bomb hit their home, sparing only two rooms. Again, she escaped serious injury when a bomb fell near her in the street, destroying surrounding buildings.

Despite all the privations brought about by the war and her own frail health, Amata concerned herself with those worse off than herself. Her charity extended to an elderly, paralyzed niece of the deceased parish priest. Since the elderly woman was unable to care for herself, Amata helped by visiting her each day to bathe her and clean her house. Until the end of the war, Amata prepared two meals for the woman each day until the invalid went to her eternal reward.

During this time, Amata was also caring for her own mother, who was sickly from a lack of proper nourishment. Amata again fell ill with a condition that provoked vomiting, which completely baffled the doctor. A cyst then developed on her left eyelid, requiring an operation to correct the eye, which was immobile. Next, she was diagnosed with tuberculosis and was ordered to enter a sanatorium, but relatives took her into their home until she was better.

A new phase in Amata's life, and that of her friend Carmen, was their meeting a Carmelite priest of the Ancient Observance, Fr. Augustine Bartolini, in 1948. It was this good priest who became her spiritual adviser and helped her to form the organization known as The Family. Amata had by this time attracted to herself a group of women who joined her frequently for prayer. This group of ten petitioned for acceptance as Third Order members of the Carmelite family and were admitted as such in February, 1957. Amata accepted the name of Amata of Jesus at her reception, a name that is on her tombstone.

Amata was already advanced in the spiritual life by means of her acceptance of suffering as the will of God, and she progressed even more rapidly under Fr. Augustine's guidance. She was especially devoted to the Blessed Sacrament, and she was grieved when her illnesses prevented her from daily reception of the Sacrament. When her health permitted, she spent hours before the Blessed Sacrament in deep contemplation.

Amata realized that she had been privileged to participate in the Lord's sufferings for the salvation of souls, and she fought gallantly against the Devil's insinuations to the contrary. She was especially devoted to the souls in purgatory and accepted her sufferings and other sacrifices for their relief. However, her charity did not extend to poor souls only, but included the living as well, especially those who were ill or poor.

The lay movement known as The Family was centered in the Carmelite house in Castellina, one of the hill towns overlooking Florence, Italy. The Family had several branches of the apostolate, each working in a different area of need.

For some years, The Family owned textile mills, which were organized on the Catholic principles of social justice outlined by the Church. The workers were brought together in the mill's chapel for daily Mass, and the Rosary was prayed during the workday. In addition, regular meetings were held to provide instructions on the Scriptures and the teachings of the Church.

To unite the members on social levels, various sporting teams were organized. Hunters belonged to the St. Martin group, and fishermen belonged to the St. Peter's group. St. Raphael was the patron of engaged couples. Young people known as Swallows kept in contact with those who had left the Church, while Samaritans looked after the sick. There were other social groups, along with enthusiastic cycling championships.

It is amazing that The Family's various branches of social and religious activities were directed by Amata and the good priest, even while she suffered so much. Although in great pain, she was driven to organize every possible apostolate that would bring glory to God. She suffered through the whole organizational process of The Family, but her goal was foremost in her mind and heart. Somehow, through the grace of God, she was able to subordinate her sufferings to the goals of the organization to assist people in their spiritual journeys, as well as those who were in dire need of The Family's services.

Suffering physically and financially all her life, Amata continued to help those in need, and through her organization she assisted countless fellow sufferers—not only those who were poor or sick, but countless others who were on the fringe of society. Those who were victims of prejudice, dishonesty, or cruel poverty were helped, as well as those who were ostracized by society, including adulterers and even lepers. God alone knows all the good that was achieved by this organization founded by Amata, who was a credit to her Carmelite family.

Toward the end, Amata was known to have said, "I'm no longer good for anything. I only know how to suffer." Yet the love of

God continued to drive her to people who needed a helping hand, a compassionate ear, or an encouraging word.

The beginning of the end came at Christmastime in 1962, when she attended services with greater fervor than usual. At this time, she was living with the Gelli family, who had offered her hospitality. In early January, she developed a severe cold that progressed with a high fever and spasms, which shook her whole body. With her body feeling as though on fire, she asked to receive the last sacraments of the Church.

The Franciscan friar who came to her bedside was amazed at her abandonment to the will of God. She lingered for a few days, assisted by members of The Family. After falling into a coma, she breathed her last on January 26, 1963, in the presence of her long-time friend, Carmen.

Her influence, which had affected so many, was also extended to one of the sons of the Gelli family, who entered Carmel and became an ordained priest working with Fr. Augustine Bartolini in directing The Family.

At the time of Amata's death, several thousand were numbered as members of The Family, which continues to bring peace and charity to those in need. †

Blessed Angela (Aniela) Salawa

1891–1922

Domestic Servant

POLAND

$\mathcal{H}$er family had limited financial resources, but Angela Salawa was taught a love of prayer and work, and a spirit of sacrifice. Born on September 9, 1881, in Siepraw, Poland, she lived at home until she was sixteen years old. She moved then to a home in Cracow, where she was employed as a domestic servant. When she was eighteen, she witnessed the peaceful and edifying death of her sister, Teresa, which so affected her spiritually that she made a firm decision to seek sanctity in a poor and humble life. By the special grace of God, she felt called to live in the state of virginal chastity.

She seems to have been contented in her position in her new home, and she engaged in an active apostolate among members of the family and many of the domestic servants in the area. She lived a peaceful and prayerful life, performing her duties with the utmost care. She was a simple soul who once said that she must master her work because, in doing so, she encountered many occasions to pray and offer sacrifices. "Outside of this," she said, "I desire nothing else in the world."

She participated with an active faith in various devotions, especially in the adoration of the Eucharist and the Way of the Cross. She was especially devoted to the Mother of God and practiced to a remarkable degree a theological life of faith, hope, and charity toward God and her neighbor.

Angela was deeply effected by the death of her mistress and her mother, in 1911, two people who meant the most to her.

She soon discovered that her spirit of humility and poverty was attuned to that of the Franciscan Order. So she decided to live the life of a Secular Order Franciscan. She was professed as a tertiary on August 6, 1913.

During World War I, she collaborated with those seeking peace. She left her domestic job to work in the hospitals of Cracow, attending and comforting the injured soldiers. So proficient and caring was she that the injured soldiers called her the "young saintly lady."

She became ill in 1917 and was forced to stop working. In one simple rented room, she spent the next five years of her life in the midst of continuous sufferings, which she offered to God for the expiation of the sins of the world, the conversion of sinners, the salvation of souls, and the missionary expansion of the Church.

She died a humble servant on March 12, 1922, in Cracow, at the age of 41, with her virtues being spread quickly throughout Poland.

Angela was beatified on August 13, 1991, during a visit by Pope St. John Paul II to Cracow. During the Mass that celebrated her beatification, St. John Paul said, among other remarks: "It exceedingly pleases me to be able to celebrate in Cracow the beatification of Angela Salawa. This daughter of Poland was born at Siepraw, and lived her remarkable life in Cracow. This city was the place of her work, her sufferings, and her development in sanctity. In the spirit of St. Francis, she showed an unusual sensitivity under the action of the Holy Spirit. Her writings [a diary] have left us considerable testimony to it."

Later, the Pope spoke about two saintly women, the Queen of heaven and Angela, when he said, "To serve God is to reign. . . . The same truth finds expression in the life of a great queen and a simple maid." †

Venerable Anita Cantieri

1910–1942

Carmelite Tertiary

ITALY

Saying that "a flower has appeared on the earth," Fr. Lawrence of St. Albert, the provincial of the Discalced Carmelites of Toscana, spoke glowingly of this Venerable. She suffered patiently, she was "all simple, all attractive, and sweet," and she presented a holy soul in the spirit of Carmel that is worthy of imitation. Although Anita Cantieri was a chosen soul, confined to bed in pain for several years, her holiness became well known. Her funeral was attended by several priests, along with a large and impressive procession of those who admired her virtues and her love of God.

Anita was born in Lucca, March 30, 1910, to David Cantieri and Annunziata Fanucchi, who were blessed by God with 12 children, all of whom, except for a brother, preceded Anita. Some of the children died in childhood, but Anita was a very healthy little girl who had a vivacious character and knew how to get her way with her siblings. In time, she received the sacraments, and at the age of six started to attend the city schools. She loved her lessons and was regularly promoted.

At the age of thirteen, she attended a school in Lucca operated by the Dorothean nuns. For this period of her life, we have precious testimonials that give us a glimpse into the early spirituality of this Venerable.

One of the nuns who taught Anita wrote that she was "an example of so many beautiful virtues. She was docile and obedient to the teachers. She was gentle, charitable, silent, helpful to her slow companions, and was often seen in prayer."

Another nun, Sr. Felicita, the principal of the school, told that Anita was silent and unnoticed, and that she learned the fine points of painting and embroidery and had a great deal of aptitude for the work. "She never lost a moment of time, but worked hard and helped her companions . . . and didn't hesitate to take upon herself problems that were not hers in order to save others from reproaches."

The sisters noticed her repeated practice of virtue. One example given by one of her teachers was the time it was raining hard at the end of the school day. Anita did not have an umbrella, so Sr. Felicita wanted to lend her one. It was a large man's umbrella, not a stylish umbrella for a young girl to carry. Anita tried her best to decline, but the nun had only to tell her to take it when Anita, in obedience, accepted it with a smile and a warm word of gratitude.

Another incident involved her daily reception of the Holy Eucharist. At a time when the Eucharistic fast began at midnight and lasted until the time of reception, Anita did not eat breakfast and went to school immediately after Mass. Since going home for breakfast would make her late for school, she preferred to continue her fast in imitation of Our Lord, who often missed His meals during the days of His public ministry.

When her mother realized that she was missing her morning meal, she prepared one each day for her, and wrapped it so that

Anita could eat it before attending school. It was noticed that this breakfast was often placed in the hands of the first poor person that Anita met along the road.

She had a great love of Jesus, so great that when her companions looked for her, they often found her in church, where she stayed a long time in communion with the Blessed Sacrament.

After a course of lectures in 1929, held by Fr. Anzuini of the Company of Jesus, Anita and her companions began working for the Apostolate of Prayer within the parish. Fr. Anzuini was well known in Italy as an apostle of the devotion to the Sacred Heart of Jesus and as a director of souls. After having listened to Anita's confession, he expressed this judgment: "This is not a common soul . . . but already very advanced in spirit."

Anita was particularly fond of working for the missions and made garments for the non-Christian children. She also appealed for mission money from her companions, the parish, and in the country.

She was also concerned for the poor who had little or no money to offer the priest after the baptism of their babies. To save them from embarrassment, she collected money and approached Sr. Felicita with the needed offering. Sister reported, "Anita would come to me and quietly give me a small sum of money. All her works of charity were performed with so much delicacy and humility that her charity passed unnoticed."

The maturity of her soul progressed to such a point that she wanted to give herself to God. From a note she wrote, we learn that Anita knew the first call of a religious vocation when she was twelve years old. During one of her excursions for the missions, she was returning home and was making a steep descent on her bicycle when the brakes failed to work.

Death seemed inevitable, but she had the presence of mind to offer herself entirely to Jesus if she escaped injury. She returned home completely unhurt and extremely happy. Since she escaped injury, she realized that God had accepted her offer.

As she grew older, her contacts with the Sisters of St. Dorothy reinforced her desire for the religious life, as did the consul-
tations with her confessor. Her parents, however, were reluctant
to lose her. They had always hoped that one of their sons would
enter the priesthood, but none seemed inclined toward that state.
Her mother, especially, tried to change Anita's mind, but the intervention of certain priests who knew Anita influenced her mother
otherwise.

At the suggestion of her father, she submitted to having a photograph taken with her long braids hanging over her shoulders.
She admitted to being uncomfortable during this process since she
considered it vain, but this was another matter of obedience.

As to the choice of a religious order, she left it entirely to her confessor, Msgr. Angelo Pasquinelli, who asked for suggestions from
members of the clergy who knew Anita. The consensus was that
Anita seemed to be contemplative and suited to the life of a Carmelite nun. The good monsignor chose for Anita the Institute of the
Tertiary Carmelite Nuns, an order founded in 1874 by Sister Teresa
Maria of the Cross, whose cause for beatification is in progress.

As to her simplicity in leaving the choice of a religious order to
another, one of Anita's friends reported this episode: "I, too, wondered which institute to enter. One day Anita told me, 'You go to
Msgr. Pasquinelli and tell him, "Monsignor, where does Jesus want
me to go?" And then you obey as if God spoke to you.' I did this
and my worry was over. I was happy as I am today."

The two friends were destined for the same convent and entered
the Corpus Domini convent in the Florentine house of the institute on May 24, 1930. On their arrival, her friend said that Anita
jumped for joy and exclaimed, "We have finally arrived!"

The convent of the Corpus Domini in Florence was the house
of probation for the aspirants of the institute, where they received
an intellectual education and spiritual formation. Here the nuns
conducted a kindergarten, and in the elementary schools taught
sewing, music, and languages. In the higher grades, for a time,

they taught commercial skills, but the convent is known in Florence above all as the Institute of Perpetual Adoration.

Anita was delighted to find that two nuns, dressed in the Carmelite mantle, alternated day and night in front of the exposed Blessed Sacrament. This pious practice, expressly instituted by the Venerable foundress, did not stop even during the years of World War II, when aerial bombardments caused destruction in the vicinity.

On the evening of Anita's entrance in the convent, Anita was asked the usual question by the superior: "Why did you come to Carmel?"

To this she replied, "To become holy as St. Teresa."

Anita adjusted well to religious life. She accepted with humility reproaches that were meant for others who were guilty of infractions, and she said nothing when others were given credit for some good deed she had performed. She wrote home: "I live a blessed life . . . and I spend so many happy days." In another letter, she confided to her mother that she suffered from a little stomach problem, which she considered insignificant.

But her health, which up to then had been excellent, started to deteriorate with weakness and intermittent fevers. The physicians who were consulted diagnosed Anita's condition as intestinal fever, what was then called Maltese fever. This was the first sign of an illness that would eventually confine her to bed until her death.

When asked how she was feeling, she hid her indisposition under a constant smile, but the color of her face revealed her sad condition. Other times she would smile and say that she was fine, since this was what Jesus wanted.

Always wanting to be of service to the community, she was permitted at times to replace someone during their time of adoration. "She seemed a seraph when before the Eucharist," one of the sisters reported. "She almost never opened a book, and passed the time with her eyes fixed on the host. . . . I have never seen her assume a comfortable position. She sat immobile without leaning against her chair."

To aid in her recovery, the good sisters sent her to a village on the outskirts of Florence, which was nestled among pleasant hills. But her condition continued to worsen.

With regret, the sisters returned her to her family, telling her to get well quickly and return to them. Anita left the convent in August 1931, after only fifteen months of conventual life. When her mother arrived to take her home, the superior said to her, "This child is an angel."

Anita accepted her deep disappointment with tears, but once again accepted this as the will of God, saying, "I feel certain that I can still give myself wholly to Jesus at home, and that I can save many souls through suffering." Her return to the convent, however, was never to be.

Anita always stayed in affectionate contact with the sisters, and on the feast day of St. Teresa of Jesus, she sent some of her simple poems to the community of Corpus Domini. In this way she was following in the footsteps of St. Teresa of Jesus and St. John of the Cross, whose poems are considered classics in the melodious Castilian language.

Although Anita's poems are not considered to be of a truly artistic nature, their content discloses the love of her heart, the feelings of her soul, and the delicacy of her charity. Through some of these poems she revealed how much it cost her to leave the religious life, but also the promptness she exercised to conform herself to the will of God, to save souls, and to aspire to attain a holy life in the world.

After her return home, the trouble that afflicted her intestines and peritoneum continued. But Anita, considering the serious response of the physician and the concern of her family, nevertheless felt the need to thank Jesus for the strength He had given her to appear serene. She frequently repeated the words, *Deo Gratias.*

In a letter to Sr. Carmelitane of the institute, Anita wrote: "I am happy that you are reaching the goal for which you strive; however, I don't envy you, because Jesus has chosen for me a mission more sublime, that of suffering."

Anita designed for herself a rule of life and of daily observances. She wrote that when she awoke in the morning, she offered the day to God with all its troubles and pain, and mentioned "an endless number of intentions." Among those she offered all for His glory were the conversion of sinners and the sanctification of souls.

Up to the eighth hour she adored the Blessed Sacrament. Every first Thursday of the month, if she was able, she visited the Blessed Sacrament. There was a time for meditation every morning, and at midday there was an examination of conscience.

In the evening, there were prayers for a happy death and another examination of conscience. Every first Saturday she spent with the Madonna of the Rosary praying and reciting the Rosary. Anita considered daily meditation an important element in her life, since it was also ordained by the Carmelite Order.

Soon Anita realized that she would never return to the institute to become a nun in the Carmelite order. But nothing prevented her from entering the Third Order Carmelites, and soon she was professed as a Discalced Carmelite tertiary on July 1, 1935. She was inspired in this decision by St. Thérèse of the Child Jesus and by her abandonment, confidence in God, and absolute fidelity in the small things that she offered in her daily life.

Anita read the works of St. Teresa of Jesus and of St. John of the Cross. Some of her poems reflect her love of these two great saints. She once wrote, "I love Carmel with a pressing love, but more than that, I love my Lord's will." Anita also knew well the recommendation of St. John of the Cross and wrote: "To reach the possession of Everything, we have to pass along the road of Nothing."

Anita was familiar with another Carmelite saint, St. Teresa Margaret Redi, whose shrine she visited in Florence. She also visited the sanctuary of the Madonna of the Carmine, which was in the care of the Carmelite fathers, and she knew well the spiritual doctrine of St. Elizabeth of the Trinity.

Two years after becoming a tertiary, Anita was enrolled in Catholic Action, and among other good deeds, she was happy to prepare children for their first Holy Communion. She was known in the organization as being a vivacious and happy person who brightened the weary acts of charity performed by herself and others.

Finally, Anita's physical condition again caused trouble with peritonitis and fevers, which kept her in bed for the next eight years until the end of her life. During this time she was cared for by her mother and her two sisters Rita and Irma. Anita regretted that she was so much trouble to them, but she submitted to the will of God, never complained, and always managed to smile, even though she was suffering intensely. Her spiritual director, Msgr. Pasquinelli, mentioned at this time her spiritual ardor, and he revealed that she knew the exact day and hour of her death.

In addition to her sufferings, Anita practiced other penances. One was to eat her meals without ever complaining about what she was fed or to express a desire for anything different. As for thirst, especially during the summer heat, she would not break her Eucharistic fast. If she asked for water, considering that her mouth was often dry, she never complained if her companion did not immediately bring it to her. Also, we are told that she used instruments of penance, some of which are still preserved as relics.

She never spoke of her sufferings, except when ordered under obedience. She was, however, honest and forthright with her doctor and was scrupulous in following the prescriptions that were ordered. In all, she was comforted more by her love of Jesus and the Blessed Virgin.

When her spiritual director, Msgr. Pasquinelli, realized that human remedies were ineffective in restoring her body to health, he decided to take her to Lourdes. The journey by train was made in September 1935. The trip was a penance for Anita, who was completely exhausted on her arrival with pains that seemed to have worsened.

However, she took part or observed all the activities, and thanked the Blessed Virgin for giving her the strength to endure her condition. She returned to Lucca very tranquil, with an expression that indicated her pains had abated somewhat.

We know that Anita wrote a number of letters during her confinement, but it is difficult to find even one in which she did not mention the Madonna or her virtues, which she endeavored to imitate. Anita felt she was always under the Blessed Mother's maternal protection, and that she was always near to help in comforting her in her painful ascent toward holiness.

The Catholic Action in which she enrolled before she became seriously ill was not forgotten. If she could not work among the poor and the sick, she would at least suffer for them and for the salvation of souls. She also became a member in the Female Association Group of St. Gemma Galgani, whose relics grace the city of Anita's birth. Heaven alone knows what graces were imparted because of Anita.

Because Anita was unable to leave her bed or house, Mass was sometimes offered in her room, much to her great satisfaction. One such Mass was offered on the feast of St. Agnes, which Anita mentioned in a letter. Anita admired this little saint for her purity and her steadfastness in enduring the tortures that preceded her martyrdom.

According to Fr. Nazzareno and her spiritual director, Anita started receiving people who asked for her prayers or who sought comfort in their trials. After a while, the visitors were so many that "there was a constant coming and going." These visitors found comfort and inspired advice. Many told of physical ailments that were small compared to the sufferings endured by Anita, yet in spite of her pains, Anita smiled and continued to offer consolations to those wearied from the troubles of the world.

A friend who sometimes cared for her reported that each time a person was about to leave, Anita would mention some consideration from her readings or her meditations, and in this way they left with a good thought. At the end of such days, she was unable to hide her exhaustion.

Anita was now enduring almost continuous vomitings, caused by a tumor that reached the stomach. For this reason, the priest who brought her Holy Communion was uncertain whether to administer the Sacarment, wondering about some unintentional irreverence. But Anita reassured him: "As soon as I feel the priest is coming with the Eucharistic Jesus, everything stops as though my stomach were enchanted by His visit. . . . There is no danger as long as the Sacrament stays in me."

In addition to all the retchings, her high temperatures produced a beautiful, rosy complexion that deceived many into thinking she was feeling better, since she was always smiling with calm and good humor. She talked to everyone and never mentioned her suffering. When asked about her condition, Anita always smiled and changed the conversation. Yet the sufferings of Anita "constituted a slow and lingering martyrdom."

During the last year of her life, Anita was met with another ailment, that of a tumor in a "delicate part of the body." The physician determined that an operation was necessary and performed the surgery without an anesthetic. He afterward reported: "In the whole time not a complaint, not a disorderly gesture was noticed."

After this operation and during the whole of her sufferings, she never accepted anything that would lessen her pains, wanting always to give the whole of her condition for the love of God and the salvation of souls. Under obedience, however, she accepted injections that were meant to prevent infection.

Finally, her heart became affected with continuous palpitations. Anita made good use of these by praying, "Dear Lord, every pulsation of my heart is a throb of love for You." The tumor was now extending its roots from the bowel to the stomach and into the trachea. A surgical intervention was necessary, to which she obediently submitted.

To the pains she already endured was added that of a spiritual nature, which was scrupulosity, in which she worried, among other difficulties, that she would not be able to die well. She mentioned,

"I strive in these assaults to make acts of trust in the love of God." She was aided during these times by Fr. Nazzareno and obeyed in blind obedience the recommendations of her spiritual director. "I resort to obedience, and then I am soothed," she said.

To all the pains previously mentioned, Anita had to endure yet three more, that of rheumatism, difficulty with the lungs, and peritonitis of the intestines. Anita was able to write a brief note to a priest, in which she mentioned, "Jesus is so good to me in letting me participate in the sufferings of the Cross."

At another time, her physician said to her that he couldn't explain her existence were it not for a miracle from God. After this, Anita remarked that her condition left her in complete abandonment to the mercy of God, since she was always in a condition of death.

Her eight years of martyrdom were now about to end. On August 23, 1942, she received the final sacraments and Viaticum— the food for the passage through death to eternal life—which she received with joy. But on August 24, the feast of St. Bartholomew the Apostle, the patron of her parish, the day she had predicted she would die, she asked her sister to arrange her hands in an attitude of prayer, since she was unable to do so herself. Then, while the feast day was being celebrated, Anita went to her heavenly reward. Her body was dressed in white, a symbol of her innocence, and in her hands a crucifix and rosary were placed.

Those who had visited her in life, and those who had heard of her spirituality, converged on the house to pray beside the body. Many mentioned that they had had the courage to return to the sacraments after speaking with Anita, while others declared that they were able to face their trials through Anita's prayerful encouragement. Great crowds visited her when she was brought to the church to receive the final blessings, while a huge procession of people, preceded by several priests, accompanied the body to the cemetery, where it was laid to rest in the tomb of her father, who had preceded her in death.

In her will, she distributed her few possessions and requested that a simple wooden cross be erected on her grave site, engraved with her date of birth and death, and for her name only the words, "*Deo Gratias.*" Her wishes were not fulfilled, since the slab of marble reads: "30–3–1910—24–VIII–1942, Anita Cantieri, Follower of Jesus on the Cross. Seeker of the heavenly church. She asked on her grave only the words *Deo Gratias.*"

Every day there are applications for relics and particles of her clothing, and for permission to pray in her room.

Anita's cause for beatification was introduced in 1977. She was declared Venerable in 1991. †

Servant of God Anna Maria Inguscio

1938–1986

Mother of Two, Adopted Mother of Many

ITALY

A husband and wife to be simultaneously considered for beati-fication are Anna Maria and Marcello Inguscio. Their story is one of unselfish love, self-sacrifice and a deep love of God and His sickly children on earth.

Anna Maria, whose family was Swiss, was born in Catania, Italy, in 1938. Little is known of her early life until we find her working in a house of the sick in Catania.

Marcello was born in Lecce, Italy, in 1934, and later stud-ied music, eventually obtaining a diploma from the Lyceum of Music. He won several competitions and in 1972 was appointed first double-bass player at Catania's Bellini Theater. Six years later, he was appointed vice director of the music school, but his musi-cal career was interrupted when Marcello had to undergo three surgical operations, which prompted him to reflect on the gift of life. The serious nature of his ordeal inspired him to promise God that if he were cured, he would dedicate himself to the care of the poor and sick.

The two first met briefly in Messina, but years later they met again in a suburb of Catania, where Anna Maria was working in the house of the sick. Their friendship gradually blossomed as they prayed together and dedicated themselves to volunteer work. There was a serious obstacle in their friendship, however, since Marcello was Catholic and Anna Maria was a Protestant Waldensian. But they came to an agreement: Marcello would study Protestant theology; Anna Maria would study Catholicism. The future they left to the will of God.

After studying Catholicism for some time, Anna Maria realized the beauty and correctness of the Catholic faith and decided to convert. The key to her conversion was a 1957 meeting in France with Fr. Abbe Pierre, a holy priest who dedicated his life to the homeless.

With the obstacle of religious orientation eliminated, Anna and Marcello decided to marry. Among the family and loved ones attending the event were forty handicapped people. The reception following the ceremony was not a typical one, since the newlyweds spent it in feeding the handicapped, who were delighted at having witnessed the beautiful ceremony and the special attention given them at the reception by the blissfully happy bride and groom.

The house the couple had established contained a room for a chapel, but since they were not permitted to retain the Holy Eucharist there, they placed a Bible in the center of the altar as an aid to meditation and prayer. Their rooms were arranged to provide a pleasant home setting for the handicapped. This was the first grassroots community known as the Mission Church-World, an organization to which they belonged.

In time the couple had two daughters, Marietta and Lucia. But they also cared for other children, who considered the Inguscios their parents. The children were raised in an intensely religious home and were accustomed to being surrounded by the seriously ill, the poor, the paralytic, and the homeless, who were always in the house.

Since the Inguscio home was already crowded with those in need, Anna Maria and Marcello, together with a few volunteers, established the Casa-Familia Puebla, where more of the needy could live in a family atmosphere. Other such houses were established to relieve the needs of the ill and crippled.

When Marcello decided that he needed more extensive training in caring for the sick, he studied for a professional nursing diploma.

When this was obtained, he continued to visit those who were confined to their homes. His patients considered him so trustworthy that he always carried with him a large number of household keys so that he could enter the homes without disturbing the sickly occupants.

Somehow, with all their busy activities, they found time to organize volunteers, who served as bearers when the sick were brought on pilgrimages to Lourdes, Fátima, and Loreto, and sometimes to Rome and Assisi. These pilgrimages were repeated many times.

Eventually, the couple took vows of poverty, chastity, and obedience, and continued their dedication to the Mission Church-World organization.

After a lifetime of dedication to the least of God's children, Anna Maria died of cancer in 1986. Marcella succumbed to a heart attack ten years later in 1996. Archbishop Luigi Bommarito of Catania took little time in opening the diocesan phase of the beatification process, and proclaimed the couple Servants of God. †

Venerable Armida Barelli

1882–1952

Cofounder of a Secular Organization

ITALY

*A*rmida Barelli was born into an affluent professional family in Milan and was educated in convent schools in Switzerland and Germany. When she was twenty-five years old, this very capable and talented young lady assumed the management of the family business after the death of her father and continued its successful operation for many years. Until she was twenty-eight years old she wondered about God's plan for her life—that is, until she met the Franciscan priest Fr. Agostino Gemelli, who became a decisive influence on her spiritual life.

That same year, she entered the Franciscan Third Order. Under this good priest's influence, she made a commitment to serve God as a layperson in the world. Her talent for organization was first demonstrated when she and Fr. Gemelli began a movement in which Italian soldiers in World War I were consecrated to the

Sacred Heart. This was expanded later to the allied armies and the populations of France, Belgium, and England.

At the same time, Cardinal Andrea Ferrari, Archbishop of Milan, invited Armida to involve herself in the young women's branch of Catholic Action. She not only became involved, but was also made head of this movement in Italy by Pope Benedict XV in 1918. She was soon known among the workers in the movement, and by those to whom they ministered, as the "great sister," a title she retained during the rest of her life. As a leader in Catholic Action, she did much to organize Italian women in politics in the troubling time after the war.

With Fr. Gemelli, she founded in 1919 an association of consecrated laywomen that would become known as the Secular Institute of Missionaries of the Kingship of Christ, but was also known simply as SIM, or Secular Institute of Missionaries. Starting with a nucleus of eleven Franciscan tertiaries, the organization grew to number some three thousand members who work in twenty countries.

The missionaries formally take vows of chastity, poverty, and obedience, but they remain seculars. As laywomen, they continue to own their own property, according to the Franciscan spirit. They are responsible for their own finances and wear ordinary secular clothing. They do not live in community, although there are times during each year when they assemble for meetings and retreats.

Both Fr. Gemelli and Armida worked diligently to gain papal approval for the organization. It was received as a Secular Institute of Pontifical Right in 1953.

Armida's years of great activity were curtailed somewhat in 1949, when she was afflicted with a bulbar paralysis that left her unable to speak. She continued to work, but gradually she became incapacitated, preventing all activity. She endured her condition for three years until her death in Milan on August 15, 1952, at the age of seventy.

Her body was entombed in the crypt of the Catholic University of the Sacred Heart in Milan. The university has recognized her efforts in helping to establish it, and for the many students she arranged to assist financially.

The Congregation for the Causes of Saints recognized Armida's holy life by issuing a *Positio Super Virtutibus* in 1993. †

Venerable Benedetta Bianchi

❦

1936–1964

Blind, Deaf, and Paralyzed Patient

ITALY

𝓑enedetta Bianchi was the second of six children born to engineer Guido Bianchi and Elsa Giammarchi in Dovadola, in the province of Forli, Italy. She was born healthy on August 8, 1936, but a drastic change took place soon after when the child hemorrhaged. Because of the seriousness of the situation, the mother felt it necessary to baptize the child, which she did with water from Lourdes.

Then, when Benedetta was three months old, she developed polio, which left her with one leg shorter than the other. Although delicate, she was a sensible and intelligent girl who loved to play with her brothers and the neighborhood children. It was not surprising that, at the age of five, at the suggestion of her mother, she began to keep a diary with simple little entries corresponding to her age. She wrote about her family, the games she played, and the beauty of nature. One entry reads: "The universe is charming. . . . How beautiful it is to live."

33

In the small Church of the Annunciation in Dovadola, little Benedetta made her First Holy Communion in May 1944. Soon after, with the terrors of World War II at their height, the Bianchi family moved to various places. When Benedetta was nine years old, they moved back to the province of Forli, where she attended the school of the Dorothean Sisters.

Because of the condition of her legs, she was forced to wear a heavy orthopedic shoe. Her classmates taunted her repeatedly. But Benedetta did not take offense at their teasing and said simply, "They speak the truth."

She loved to study and spent whole hours practicing at the piano. The remnants of polio, in the meantime, produced a defect in her spine that was to cause extreme pain, and in addition she began to experience a loss of hearing.

After the family's move to Sirmione in 1951, on the beautiful Lake Garda, Benedetta began studying at the institute and discovered within herself a new strength of spirit. In the school paper she wrote, noting her lack of hearing: "Perhaps someday I will hear nothing of which the others speak, but I will listen to the voice of my soul, and this one is the true way that I must follow."

For some time, Benedetta was required to wear an orthopedic brace around her torso to prevent a deformity of her back. This produced a great deal of pain and discomfort, but she was still known to declare, "How wonderful is life!"

After her third year at the institute, in the autumn of 1953, she moved to Milan to attend the university. She was then seventeen years old. At the suggestion of her father, she registered in the school of physics, but after only a month she was convinced that she was more inclined to study medicine, saying, "I have undertaken the new study with ardor. I have always dreamed of being a doctor. I want to live, to fight, to sacrifice myself for all men."

Her deafness, however, became more acute, so that she was accompanied by her friend, Ana, who warned her when the professor was calling upon her. Once when she asked the professor to repeat a question in writing, because of her loss of hearing, he threw a book against the door and shouted, "A deaf doctor has never been seen."

Benedetta rose quietly, picked up the book, and in a soft voice asked his pardon. Despite the professor's attitude, she was permitted to continue her studies. She was someone to admire, as she went from class to class, leaning on a cane for support, the result of the polio that left her partially paralyzed.

Finally, when the deafness was almost complete, she learned the name of the disease: Recklinghausen, or diffuse neurofibromatosis, a rare genetic disorder characterized by incurable, progressively developing non-cancerous tumors of the nervous system. The disease assaults, among other functions, the nerves affecting vision, hearing, and speech. It was suggested that an operation might relieve some of the symptoms.

For this she was forced to interrupt her studies. She said to a friend, "Only heaven knows what this costs me. But patience; the important thing is not to lose the peace of my soul."

In June 1957 she submitted to the surgical procedure, which was a failure. It did, however, leave half her face paralyzed. In preparation for this operation, her head was shaved. She responded that she felt "like a lamb before a shearer. . . . I have asked the Savior that I may always be a little lamb in His hands."

When she returned to school, she happily passed the examinations of medical pathology and surgical pathology. Once again, however, her studies were interrupted when, in 1959, at the age of twenty-three, she required an operation on the spine. This operation was also a failure; she lost all feeling in her legs, and was forced to remain in bed for the rest of her life.

Recklinghausen disease was again active when, little by little, she lost the sense of taste, and then the sense of smell. She found comfort in this ordeal by confiding herself to the care of the Blessed Mother and to the mercy of God.

Benedetta was not a sad patient, nor did she feel sorry for herself. In fact, she accepted her disabilities with such joy that many who visited her room found comfort in her presence and her advice. One who often visited revealed, "Benedetta made us forget our troubles. All day, in turn, we communicated with her. We laughed, we sang together, and we recited Vespers." In her brief writings, she revealed her thirst and hunger for God, thanking Him for the gift of life.

Another ailment visited her in October 1962, when she lost almost all her teeth. Before this took place, the hospital of the Unitalsi took her to Lourdes. Benedetta was happy and said, "I am going to receive the blessings of the heavenly Mother." For her the miracle of Lourdes was the discovery of her authentic vocation of the Cross. "I have found more than ever before the value of my condition, and I desire to conserve it."

Months later, on Ash Wednesday, February 1963, she underwent her last operation in the hospital of Milan. This produced a tremendous suffering. Benedetta remarked, "I am in the Garden of Olives. What fatigue, but I accept this with joy." She embraced her situation, as one would expect of a future saint.

She went a second time to Lourdes, but this time to pray for others because, she declared, "Charity is to live for others."

Then, in addition to her paralysis and deafness, she experienced the loss of sight and a difficulty in speech, the other symptoms of the disease. At first, when she began to lose her sight, she would put her hand on another's to "read" the letters of the alphabet. Then she began to learn Braille and responded to questions with words that were considered spiritual gems. She once wrote, "The greatest prodigy of all is love. . . . Jesus is with me and my sufferings, and He gives me peace in solitude and light to my blindness. He smiles at me and accepts my cooperation with Him."

A Dominican sister who was at Benedetta's side during her period of recuperation, and during the time that she developed the unexpected blindness, gave this testimony:

"I never found another person who knew how to support so many sufferings as did Benedetta. In her room of pain she was always radiating joy. Whoever visited her found in her light and warmth, a comfortable calmness, which invited all to do good. Something divine was perceived by those who approached her. She was the goal of many visitors, mainly students who requested advice from her."

Others observed that, as her condition grew worse, the more the room filled with people.

Her father, on the other hand, did not want to learn Braille or sign language, and for some time he would only enter Benedetta's room, stay for a moment or two, and then leave. One day, Benedetta signaled that she wanted to speak with her father. At first he resisted, but his wife rebuked him with strong words, which compelled him to visit his daughter's bedside.

He put his hand on hers, and she responded: "Daddy, this is your hand that works so hard for us."

To this he replied, "Yes, I work, but I am glad to do it for all of you." He then left the room crying.

Next, Benedetta called for her mother, and in a soft, sweet voice, corrected her for the remarks she had made to her husband. "Mama, when you pray, 'forgive us our trespasses,' don't you know what you are saying? Do you really think that rebukes do much good? When a person makes a mistake, make him feel even more that you love him."

Benedetta's mother recalled the incident later in life: "I was struck dumb. . . . She saw what we didn't see. Her sensitivity had become more acute with her illness."

During the morning of January 23, 1964, while Benedetta was living in Sirmione, she asked her mother to read the *Act of Oblation to Merciful Love* that had been written by her favorite saint, St. Thérèse of the Child Jesus. No sooner had she finished reading than the mother looked outside and saw a white rose blooming in the garden despite the winter cold. Benedetta regarded it as a "very sweet sign." Shortly afterward, she passed to her heavenly reward.

This beautiful soul had experienced the effects of polio, suffered a partial paralysis of her face, experienced deafness and blindness, as well as the loss of most of her teeth, the sense of taste and smell. She endured painful and ineffectual operations. Yet she suffered from these conditions for the salvation of souls, and accepted her condition with joy and peace.

In recognition of her pure soul, she was soon given the title of Servant of God by the episcopal authorities upon opening her cause for canonization. She was declared Venerable in December 1993.

In her brief life of twenty-seven years, she seems to have disclosed to the world a joy of life to the burdened and hope to the desperate. Her tomb in the Dominican Church of the Annunciation at Dovadola, in her native country, is only a short distance from Forli. It is there that a multitude of devotees visit her bronze tomb that was fashioned by the master, Angelo Biancini.

Benedetta's letters and reflections have been published and translated into many languages. She now awaits beatification, which her countless devotees pray will be very soon. ✝

Venerable Carla Ronci

1936–1970

Tailor

ITALY

*C*arla Ronci was a beautiful girl who loved life and people. The many photographs we have of her show her smiling broadly, betraying a joyous and winsome personality. She was the same during her childhood in Torre Pedrena as the daughter of Mario and Iolanda Ronci, merchants who operated a fruit and vegetable shop. She was born on April 11, and in time received her First Holy Communion and the Sacrament of Confirmation.

Her contemporaries remembered her as being lively and mischievous, gentle and affectionate, strong-willed, polite and sometimes irritable. Her third-grade teacher remembered her as being an exemplary pupil, kind, affectionate, good, and industrious. But Carla remembered her early childhood in another way. She once wrote:

"I am casting my mind back to my past—but I cannot hide it from you that it hurts me to remember what happened in those days, especially up until the age of fourteen. What sins I committed and what bad deeds I did. At a very early age I began going to dances and the cinema, reading naughty magazines and getting into bad company. You can well imagine what my soul was like under the guidance of such teachers, and what would have happened unless the Lord, in His divine mercy, had not plucked me from the clutches of evil, for that was just where I had sunk. . . .

"Up until the age of ten, I have a vague recollection of being a little girl who was neither very good nor very naughty. Over the next four years however, I sinned and I realized that I was responsible for what I was doing, because the Lord made himself felt by continually pricking my conscience."

Carla remembered her condition at the age of fourteen: "I yearned after all I thought might satisfy the void and anxiety within me; I sought to dull my senses with one amusement after another, but all in vain." Her confessor, Fr. Napoleone, reported that in spite of Carla's negative opinion of her early life, he is convinced that she "kept her moral innocence intact."

Then came the Holy Year of 1950 and her "spiritual revival." It was during this year that Carla met a group of Ursuline nuns, who were devoted to helping abandoned children and the poor. This meeting so impressed the young Carla that she felt she should undertake the same apostolate, especially after attending a mission in her parish church that changed her life. Her mother wrote:

"That evening, I saw my Carla return transformed; in her I immediately discerned a rare joy mixed with a calm sadness. . . . Up until then she had loved enjoyment, trips, reading magazines, dancing and films. Later, many other things were to disappear from her everyday life. She started going to Mass more frequently; she took sacraments more seriously and treated me, her daddy, and her little sister much better. Her requests for cinema money were more and more infrequent, and she became more and more open toward others."

Following school, Carla was sent to study tailoring. She became skillful and worked for several years at this profession, also sewing clothes for herself and members of the family. Because of her skills, she was said to have dressed elegantly in modest fashions made of simple fabrics. Her free time from work was spent either in her parents' shop or engaged in helping with the activities of Catholic Action.

Also, during the Holy Year, Carla began to keep a diary, from which we learn the progress of her spirituality and the degree of perfection that she attained. We also learn that she was consecrated to the Blessed Mother, according to the method of St. Louis Grignon De Montfort, during the year 1956.

Remembering her attraction for the Ursuline Order, she entered into the aspirancy on February 3, 1958, at the age of twenty-two. Unfortunately, she spent only four months with the nuns before she returned home because of her health, and with the decision of the nuns that she did not have a vocation to their order. The return home was, no doubt, very disappointing for Carla, who accepted it as the will of God.

She immediately returned to her usual activities with Catholic Action and opened a small school of sewing. Still feeling inclined to join a religious organization, Carla looked about for an order that would accept her as a tertiary, or auxiliary member. Her prayers were answered when she was introduced to the Institute of the Handmaids of the Mother of Mercy, to which she applied on January 6, 1961.

She was accepted into the institute, and while in the motherhouse for training, she attended several courses of study and was admitted to religious profession on January 6, 1963. This allowed her to return home as a consecrated layperson. At the time she wrote: "I am now the bride of Jesus."

But all was not joy and gladness. Difficulties soon arose for Carla when she experienced what she called "the Night of the Spirit." She was assailed by evil stirrings, temptations, discouragement, a little moodiness, slight depressions, fears, and obstacles. But according to her program of "not giving in" and "marching on," in time the ordeal passed, and she was restored to serenity and the happy disposition that everyone admired.

She was soon permitted by her spiritual director to make a vow of chastity, and the following year she was permitted to make a vow of poverty, dedicating herself to praying for priestly vocations and for missionaries. She was to write in her diary, "For you, Jesus, will I live, I will love, I will suffer."

Returning to her previous activities with Catholic Action, she rode to and from her various assignments first on a bicycle, then a wasp (a motorized vehicle), and then a 500 Fiat. Photographs of her on these motorized bikes show her smiling proudly in her possession of these "modern" and convenient means of transportation. In addition to other activities, she prepared children for their First Holy Communion and taught catechism to both small and large classes of children.

She also directed sporting events for them, from ball games to boating. And in a demonstration of her happy outlook on life, she also acted in a comedy. Because of her dedication and hard work, she was also elevated to various positions of responsibility.

She was elected district leader in charge of several parishes. She was a youth leader, a Young People's and Juniors' Leader, and a section leader. In addition to her work for Catholic Action, teaching catechism, and planning parish festivals, she was also very concerned about religious vocations, praying fervently for this intention.

Someone who knew Carla during these years wrote: "All the virtues were to be found in Carla. . . . She tried to immerse herself in meditation and contemplation. Her conversation was gay, quiet, and serene; God's presence within her would shine through. Just to meet her was a tonic to one's spirit; you would feel uplifted and encouraged because Carla was the living outworking of the Gospel. She had no fear of suffering; whatever difficulties came her way she would accept with joy. She had the real mature joy of a soul hungering for God, prepared to drop all else in order to possess Him alone."

Mrs. Teresa Dotti, who also knew Carla, wrote of her: "In speaking with her, one felt in the presence of someone not of this earth. . . . Once we found her in the workshop helping a child with his schoolwork. She looked changed to me. She was still very beautiful but thinner and, I would say, above all more mature as she grew in the stature of Jesus Christ.

"She welcomed us with great joy, and while she was showing us round her workshop, she told us of her apostleship. . . . On the way home we felt great joy. My friend likened it to a spiritual-retreat experience."

During the summer of 1969, she experienced the first symptoms of the condition that would claim her life. Although she felt a great need to rest, she continued helping her mother at home and in the shop, as well as continuing her parish work. An obstinate cough developed, then pains in the chest, fever, and severe discomfort, all of which were diagnosed as a pulmonary tumor. During the early part of 1970, she began another diary, in which she described her condition and her trust in the help of God to endure whatever He had in store for her.

She was taken to the hospital of St. Orsola in Bologna on January 21, 1970, which was run by her beloved Ursuline Order. She endured a long series of examinations and tests and wrote in her diary, "Lord, you can no longer suffer in your own body, so take mine to continue your Passion and Redemption."

After a month, since there was nothing they could do to restore her to health, she was sent home, but was soon taken to Villa Maria, a nursing home in Rimini. She died there after praying aloud and saying, "Here he comes . . . Jesus is coming . . . He is smiling at me." She died on April 2, 1970, at the age of thirty-four.

Her funeral was attended by her confessor, several priests, and all those who admired her and her works of charity. Her confessor explained why he had used the liturgy of the angels, despite the fact that the parish was in mourning. He also spoke of the saintliness of her life and of the huge legacy of goodness, faith, charity, hope, and purity she was leaving behind her. He also presented her to the congregation as "an authentic angel." Afterwards, she was buried in the cemetery at Rimini.

Commemorative services were held for a number of years, and biographies were written. Because of all the attention given to her, newspapers and magazines also became interested. Eventually, eighty different biographies appeared.

Only twelve years after her death, the cause of Carla Ronci's beatification was introduced in 1982. She was declared Venerable by Pope St. John Paul II on July 7, 1997. †

Servant of God Carolina Bellandi Palladini

1895–1986

Lover of the Poor

ITALY

*C*arolina Bellandi Palladini was born into a humble family of peasant farmers in the village of St. Lorenzo (Florence), in the beautiful region of Mugello, on May 17, 1895. Hers was a deeply religious family, and she quickly absorbed the sturdy religious ideals of her relatives. As with most of the peasants at the time, she was denied a proper education, attending school for only three years. And as with all people of her station, she was obliged to work in the fields and help with the housekeeping, which she was happy to do.

Unlike many who aspired to the religious life, Carolina wanted to marry, which she did, to Olinto Palladini in 1919, when she was twenty-four years old. She and her husband wanted a large family. They implored heaven with prayers, penances, and pilgrimages, but unfortunately they were denied the joy of having children.

In the region of Mugello at that time, the spirit of St. Francis of Assisi was inspiring many to dedicate themselves to the aid of the poor through their association with the Franciscan Third Order. Carolina was inspired to follow the ideals of the order and joined as a tertiary, keeping the rule carefully for the rest of her life.

She moved to Florence with her husband, where they were employed for seven years until the great economic crisis of 1929. While employed, Carolina used her extra time to attend services at the Church of the Annunciation. Apparently, Carolina and Olinto lived on the outskirts of Florence, since she had to walk a great distance to the church. In the afternoon, she occupied herself in Eucharistic adoration and in cleaning the church of the Calasanziane nuns.

Empowered by her love of the Eucharist and contemplative prayer, Carolina was led to a ministry that was badly needed. One day in 1935, while crossing a poor section of St. Frediano in Florence, she came upon some boys playing noisily in the square. She questioned them and was horrified to learn that none of them had received their First Holy Communion. She also learned that this was due to poverty and their families' lack of interest.

She approached the families, offering to pay all the expenses involved. The instructions for the ceremony were to be provided by the Cappuccini Fathers of Montughi.

The first group of children received their First Holy Communion on January 6, 1936. Everything for the occasion was supplied, from the clothing to a sit-down breakfast and reception. Thus was the Work of the First Communions born.

Some of those who received their first Holy Communion that day went on to serve in this apostolate. One group after another repeated the ceremony. Finally, in 1950, Fr. Stanislaus Livi assumed the management of the Work of the First Communions, which spread to other cities throughout Italy and Sardinia.

Twenty thousand are said to have approached the sacrament through the Work of the First Communions, with many of the children addressing the Servant of God as "Mother Carolina." It was a name she richly deserved, since she loved them as she would have loved the children she never had.

But how did Carolina obtain the money for the ceremonies? At first, since she had little money, it seems apparent that she collected the money, little by little, from interested parties, and those who eventually helped her in the work. When questioned about the amount of money needed to clothe so many children and supply for the parties afterward, Carolina simply replied: "The bank of Jesus is a large one. Monies are never lacking there. Only hearts are lacking."

The Work of the First Communions continued until about the year 1960, when there was a worsening in the economic conditions of the region. Carolina was now almost seventy years old. She was in good health, and wanted to do more for the Church.

After the Second Vatican Council, when there was a crisis in faith and vocations, the cloistered monasteries, too, were suffering. Carolina realized this and approached the Monastery of the Clausura to ask them for prayers and to see how she could help them. With more and more nuns leaving convents to participate in social work, Carolina realized the need for these houses of prayer to continue as before.

Meanwhile, donations to the nuns was such that some of them were considering leaving the cloister to work outside for their financial needs. It was then that Carolina began another apostolate. She would financially help the cloistered nuns so they could remain in their monasteries to pray for the needs of the church.

Once again, withdrawals were made from the "Bank of Jesus," which, needless to say, was greatly appreciated by the nuns. However, it was not only the Monastery of the Clausura that was helped by Carolina. After her death, monasteries throughout the region gave testimonials of Carolina's help and inspiration.

At the age of ninety-one, Carolina was still active in helping the nuns. In December 1986, while she was busy collecting funds for them, she was badly injured in a street accident. She was taken to the hospital at Prato, where she stayed for ten days until her death on December 27. Before she died, she greeted all her visitors with a smile, and happily bid them farewell, saying, "Goodbye until paradise."

Carolina's love of the Eucharist, and the Franciscan spirit that inspired her to help the needy, were quiet activities and mostly hidden ones. Her early life was modest, as was the remainder of her life, lived in helping youngsters and God's chosen ones. She was humble, too, as revealed by her statement, "If God had not held me in His hands, I don't know what sins I would have committed."

Carolina's love of God and her advanced spirituality were recognized by the Franciscan Order. They opened her cause for beatification on October 18, 2001. ✝

Servant of God Catherine de Hueck Doherty

~

1896–1985

Founder of Friendship House

RUSSIA-CANADA

Since she was a lover of God's poor and those who experienced racial injustice, Catherine de Hueck Doherty was determined to correct these situations. In so doing she developed a deeply spiritual life that has placed her well on the way to attaining the honors of the altar.

She was born Catherine Kolyschkine in Nizhny-Novgorod, Russia, on August 15, 1896, and was baptized Orthodox. In her devout, aristocratic family she enjoyed all the comforts and advantages of her home. But she was also instructed in her faith and lived a deeply religious existence, which meant helping the poor and recognizing Christ in all she encountered.

At the age of only fifteen, Catherine felt prepared to make a serious commitment and married her cousin, Boris de Hueck. Their early years together were interrupted by the start of World War I, when Boris was called to the Russian front as an engineer. Catherine was to serve her country as a nurse.

Then, the Russian Revolution changed their lives forever. Many members of their family were killed by the Bolsheviks, which forced the couple to flee for their lives. First they emigrated to England, then in 1921 they journeyed to Canada, where their son George was born. The poverty they experienced proved a hardship on their living conditions and on their marriage. After they separated, the Church saw fit to annul the union.

Catherine's financial condition improved when it was discovered that she was a talented speaker. She traveled throughout North America on a lecture tour, but she kept remembering the promise she had made to God during the dangerous time of the revolution: that she would give her life to Him. With the renewal of this promise, her apostolate began.

In the 1930s, she provided for her son and then sold all she had to live a hidden life in the slums of Toronto, caring for the poor and destitute. Her intention was to preach the gospel by living a simple life according to the spirituality of St. Francis of Assisi. Inspired by her dedication, others soon joined her, and the Friendship House was formed.

Members begged for food and clothing, which was distributed to the poor. They gave classes and even distributed a newspaper called *The Social Forum*, which was based on the social encyclicals of the Church.

Unfortunately, unfounded rumors were spread about Catherine, which forced the closing of the Friendship House in 1936. Although greatly disappointed, she left Toronto, but her efforts on behalf of the poor were soon recognized when she was invited to open a Friendship House in Harlem in New York City, which she did two years later. Here she was able to help African-Americans and was horrified at the way they were treated in society. She gave many a lecture against this discrimination.

Although she was supported and encouraged by Cardinal Patrick Hayes and Cardinal Francis Spellman, she experienced difficulties with members of her staff, who voted against her in matters she considered essential to the apostolate. Because of this opposition, she stepped down as director general in January 1947.

Catherine had married the well-known American journalist Eddie Doherty in 1943 and moved with him to Combermere, Ontario, Canada, after her resignation from Friendship House. She still felt the urge to help the needy and was soon busy helping those in need in the Combermere area. She began to serve as a nurse and then added various charitable works to her already busy schedule. With her husband she established a newspaper, *Restoration*, and began giving classes for the lay apostolate.

In February 1951, under the guidance of their spiritual director, Fr. John Callahan, Catherine and Eddie consecrated themselves to Mary according to the teachings of St. Louis de Montfort. The Blessed Mother was to be the inspiration for their new apostolate, Madonna House. Men and women were again attracted to their work, and the organization grew.

Later that year, in October 1951, Catherine was in Rome, where she met Papal Secretary Msgr. Giovanni Montini, the future Pope Paul VI. He encouraged Catherine and her followers in their work and suggested that they consider making a permanent commitment.

Three years later, on April 7, 1954, Catherine, Eddie, and their followers made promises of poverty, chastity, and obedience under the guidance of their spiritual director, Fr. John Callahan. The next year, Catherine and her husband went a step further, when they promised to live a celibate life.

Graces were showered upon the community. Lay men and women, as well as some priests, asked to join Madonna House to live in the atmosphere of Christian family. The group begged for their needs and distributed the rest. Six years later, on June 8, 1960, the fledgling community received the Church's approval. Their organization was soon recognized by bishops throughout the world, who invited them to open houses in their countries, even in Catherine's native Russia.

Catherine's view of the apostolate was the law of love, and she often said, "The essence of our apostolate is love—love of God poured out abundantly for others."

Some twenty-five years after the official recognition of her organization, and after fifty years of working among the poor, Catherine died on December 14, 1985, following a lengthy illness. She was deeply mourned by all who knew her, especially those members of the foundation who were now established in cities around the world. †

Servant of God Cleonilde Guerra

1922–1949

Catechist

ITALY

$\mathcal{B}$orn to Giulio and Laure Guerra in San Potito (Ravenna), Cleonilde, from early childhood, was somewhat sickly after having been stricken with bronchial pneumonia. She bore her pain in silence and invited her mother to unite with her in offering the sufferings to Our Lord. Cleonilde loved to read and had a preference for the Gospels and the lives of the saints, especially that of St. Thérèse of the Child Jesus and St. Gemma Galgani.

Encouraged by her parish priest, she was attracted to Christian virtues and was particularly interested in helping with parish activities.

At the age of sixteen, she felt drawn to the religious life. But because of the opposition of her father she did not enter. Instead, she began a close relationship with the Handmaids of the Sacred Heart of the Dying Jesus. The nuns encouraged her vocation, but she felt obliged to delay her entrance. However, when she was twenty-one, she entered the novitiate of the order in Lugo.

Unfortunately, a recurrence of her childhood ailment, bronchial pneumonia, made it necessary for her to leave the convent. This disappointment brought on a severe depression, which was treated by a priest named Fr. Savorini, who convinced her that the religious life was not God's will for her. When her peace of mind was restored, Cleonilde began once again to work for the parish and became a militant worker in Catholic Action.

After World War II, and the return of the people to San Potito, Cleonilde showed an untiring spirit in her parish work for the moral and spiritual reconstruction of the people. She loved to teach and had a special preference for small children who were preparing for their First Holy Communion. She also worked with the older children who were preparing for the Sacrament of Confirmation.

Cleonilde died at the age of twenty-seven at San Potito on May 19, 1949, with a reputation of great holiness. The Congregation for the Causes of Saints has accepted the petition for her beatification. †

Venerable Concepta Bertoli

1908–1956

Paralyzed Invalid

ITALY

Concepta Bertoli had been a healthy little girl when she was born in the village of Mereto di Tomba, near the city of Udine in northeastern Italy on April 14, 1908. Her first sixteen years were spent in school and in helping in the fields, but toward the end of her sixteenth year, she developed a form of arthritis that began to deform her body. Gradually, she was completely immobilized.

Her teeth became clenched and her jaws locked, permitting only liquids to enter her mouth. Her body then became twisted in an awkward position. For the next thirty-one years, Concepta remained in that position, enduring all manner of discomfort and pain. Her pitiful condition became well known, so that she was referred to as the living crucifix of Mereto di Tomba.

Concepta accepted her affliction as coming from the hand of God, and because of her admiration of St. Francis of Assisi, she became a Franciscan tertiary in 1940. Ten years later, her physical condition became even more complicated when she became completely blind. This condition remained for the last eight years of her life.

From the very onset of her condition, she repeated often that she accepted her cross and her pain as did Jesus on Calvary. Her sufferings, she revealed, were endured for missionaries, priests, and sinners. Yet despite these sufferings, she remained serene, pleasant, and without complaint.

So confidently did she believe in the will of God for her that she once revealed:

"I don't have enough breath to thank the Lord, who has put me under these conditions. I can do so much good here on my bed. The Lord entrusts to each a place and a mission. To me He has given this bed. I am happy. Suffering without resignation is awful; but, if there is resignation, pain is nothing."

Since she could not be a missionary, she also revealed: "I am a missionary of pain."

When Concepta was thirty, she was taken on a stretcher to Lourdes, a place she had always wanted to visit. But she made it known that she would not ask for a miracle of healing—only the grace to endure her sufferings. While in front of the cave of apparitions, she asked for another grace: that she might be able to communicate better, since the position of her teeth and the rigidity of her jaws prevented clear speech.

When the twenty-fifth anniversary of the onset of her affliction drew near, she wanted it to be observed in some way. She noted that people usually celebrate a silver anniversary with the ringing of bells and a party. The bells did, indeed, ring joyously on December 24, 1949, the twenty-fifth anniversary. Her "party" was a beautiful holy Mass marking the onset of her crucifixion.

Two years later, her great wish was realized when she was taken on a stretcher to the Holy House of Loreto. One gets the impression from the account of the visit that Concepta's blindness might have receded a little to permit a little viewing of the Holy House. This is speculated since it is noted that, upon leaving Loreto, she "became blind again." But Concepta, as always, accepted the will of God and made it known: "I have lost the sight of the eyes, but I have the eyes of faith."

Concepta told her family in January 1956 that she would die within the year. Then she added, "But I am happy because I will go with the Lord." She died at Mereto di Tomba on March 11, 1956, and was buried in the parish church. An inscription on the marble of her tomb reminds one that the pains endured by this holy woman were offered to God for priests, missionaries, and sinners. It also mentions that Concepta was always pleasant and blessed by God.

In the city of Udine, the informative process for her cause of be-atification was begun in 1969, a mere thirteen years after her death. The next action in the process was made by the Congregation for the Causes of Saints in 1994. The Vatican has since issued a decree, citing the heroic virtues of Concepta Bertoli on April 25, 2001. †

Servant of God Dorothy Day

1897–1980

Founder of Catholic Worker Movement

UNITED STATES

*A*lmost immediately after her death, controversy arose as to whether Dorothy Day should be presented for possible canonization. After all, Dorothy had been a communist, had had a number of love affairs, had aborted a baby, and had spent thirty days in jail for picketing in front of the White House on behalf of women's right to vote. She had been arrested an additional six times in support of various civil rights, the last in 1973 for demonstrating on behalf of the United Farm Workers in Fresno, California.

She had also engaged in a common-law marriage and had a baby without benefit of marital vows. Her conversion after the birth of her baby, and her virtuous life since then, as well as her tireless work among the poor, were seen by Cardinal John O'Connor as the stuff of saints. It was he who introduced her cause.

To anyone who knew her in her earliest years, the suggestion that she would someday be presented for canonization would have been harshly ridiculed and loudly mocked. But to those who knew her in her latter years, canonization was regarded as a definite foregone conclusion of a life of complexity and virtue, which has inspired many to prayer and action for social justice.

Dorothy's interesting life began in San Francisco, where her family was devastated by the 1906 San Francisco earthquake. Her father, John Day, a journalist, lost his home and his job. When Dorothy was eight years old, the family moved to a small apartment situated over a tavern on Chicago's South Side. Here they lived in very poor circumstances until the father secured a job as a sports editor on a small Chicago paper.

Now, having a steady income, they were able to move to better housing. Dorothy's father, of Irish ancestry, was also a racetrack enthusiast, who later became a steward and a partner at Hialeah racetrack in Florida. He showed little affection toward his children and had little or no interest in religion. Dorothy's mother, Grace Satterlee Day, who was of English ancestry, also had little need for religion. Neither parent attended church services.

Dorothy was raised mostly in Chicago and began to read at the age of four. She first became interested in religion when she found a Bible in the attic and began reading it, confessing later that she understood very little, but that she had a feeling of devotion while reading it.

Dorothy was an excellent student. She did so well at Waller High school at the age of sixteen that she was awarded a scholarship to the University of Illinois at Urbana. After hearing one professor speaking of religion as something for the weak, Dorothy, in her youthful arrogance, decided she was strong and therefore had no need of it either. She "ceased to believe and started to swear quite consciously" and proudly professed to be an atheist.

But pride was put aside when it came to her income. Forced to work, she washed dishes at the YWCA, did household chores for three different families, living in each so she could conveniently take care of the children. She scrubbed floors, washed clothes, and did other chores, which she later described as "smothering work."

At the age of eighteen, she left college and moved to New York, where she confessed to having led a carefree life, "doing for the first time exactly what I wanted to do." With the ambition to become a journalist, but without a degree or experience, she found it impossible to find work in the larger newspapers and was forced to take what work she could. This led her to becoming a regular correspondent for the left-wing publications the *Call* and the *New Masses*.

She was now able to promote the controversial issues of the day, including women's rights, birth control, and so-called "free love"— a euphemism of that time for sexual promiscuity. She was especially drawn to those who were trying to change the country, including labor unions and picketers. She was also attracted to and enjoyed the company of the leading writers of her day, including Eugene O'Neill.

Her "carefree life" at the age of twenty involved being arrested after picketing on behalf of women's right to vote. One of the main impressions she would always remember of this experience were the many kindnesses shown her by the incarcerated prostitutes. During this prison stay, Dorothy read the Bible, taking particular comfort in the Psalms.

Her "carefree life" also included her interest in communistic ideals, for which she attended a number of meetings. It also included being involved in a series of love affairs. After becoming pregnant during one of them, she had an illegal abortion. This was to cause her deep regret for the rest of her life.

She married but once, and that to a man about whom little is known except that he had been married eight times. She journeyed with him to Europe, began drinking heavily, and separated from him on her return to the States. The marriage had lasted less than a year. To eke out a living between these episodes, Dorothy worked for a time as a clerk in a library, as a restaurant cashier, a proofreader, and even as a clerk in a Montgomery Ward store.

Around the year 1926, after her failed marriage, she engaged in a common-law-marriage to a committed atheist, Forster Batterham, and lived with him on Staten Island. Forster was a biologist and an anarchist. As a result of this association, Dorothy once again found herself pregnant. This time she decided to have the baby.

It was during this pregnancy that she began to pray almost constantly, not on her knees, but while walking and doing her work. She read from the *Imitation of Christ* and often held the rosary someone had given her the year before. Of the Rosary, she said, "Maybe I did not say it correctly, but I kept on saying it because it made me happy." She also began to make visits to the Catholic chapel, where she "prayed for the gift of faith."

The baby's arrival in July of 1927 was a cause of great happiness. Dorothy wrote in her diary that, at her daughter's birth, "spring was upon us. My joy was so great that I sat up in bed in the hospital and wrote an article for the *New Masses* about my child, wanting to share my joy with the world." She named the child Tamara, which in Hebrew means "little palm tree." She gave her the middle name Teresa, for the great St. Teresa of Ávila, whose autobiography had impressed the new mother.

Soon afterward, Dorothy was determined to have the child and herself baptized Catholic. She took instructions in the faith and was then met with a huge problem. She dearly loved Forster, but her determination to be baptized conflicted sharply with his views and their immoral situation. Since she loved the Church more, she put aside her heartbreak and left him.

Tamara and Dorothy were soon baptized. Dorothy wrote: "When one has a child, life is different. Certainly I did not want my child to flounder as I had often floundered, without a rule of life, and instruction. . . . I wanted my child to believe, and if belonging to a church would give her so inestimable a grace as a faith in God and the companionable love of the saints, then the thing to do was to have her baptized a Catholic."

Dorothy's life was changed from then on. One day, while Dorothy was in Washington, D.C., she visited the unfinished Shrine of the Immaculate Conception near the the Catholic University of America and prayed in the crypt. "There I offered up a special prayer, a prayer which came with tears and anguish, that some way would open up for me to use what talents I possessed for my fellow workers, for the poor."

In time, she met a man named Peter Maurin, who was quite unlike the other men who had previously entered her life. He was somewhat older than she. He was a writer of dogmatic material and a member of a brotherhood of men who taught the children of the poor, performed charitable works, and shunned honors and privileges. He was a man of high principles who shared Dorothy's vision of changing the dismal contemporary American scene.

Later, Dorothy was to declare that Peter's "spirit and ideas" were totally essential to the rest of her life. It was he whom she regarded as the cofounder of her newspaper, *The Catholic Worker*, in which she promulgated her religious beliefs.

The Catholic Worker's first edition in May of 1933 consisted of twenty-five hundred printed copies. By 1936, one hundred fifty thousand copies were being printed. Enthusiastic young people sold copies for one cent, but if sales were disappointing, they gave the copies away, leaving some of them in doctor's offices and on buses and streetcars. Soon the editors were receiving mail from throughout the world.

In addition to promoting her religious beliefs through the paper, Dorothy used it to declare her adherence to a neutral pacifism during all the wars of her lifetime. Like Gandhi, she struggled to build a spirit of nonviolence. During her lifetime, Dorothy wrote more than four hundred articles for her publication, which can now be read on the Internet. She also wrote an autobiography and a number of books, and she kept a diary that has been of great benefit to biographers.

With *The Catholic Worker* firmly established, Dorothy, with the inspiration and help of Peter Maurin, opened a "House of

Hospitality" in the slums of New York that would feed the hungry and house the homeless. This was begun in 1939, when they rented an eight-dollar-a-month apartment near Tompkins Square. Dorothy wrote that it was a "rat-ridden place, heatless and filthy, abandoned even by slum dwellers."

It was, of course, cleaned, tidied, and made livable. Other homes were needed, since people were being evicted everywhere.

"We had to find other apartments, help get relief checks for them, borrow pushcarts and move them. . . . Neighbors came in needing clothes and we had to go to friends and readers begging for them. . . . We cooked, cleaned, wrote, went out on demonstrations to distribute literature, got out mimeographed leaflets, answered a tremendous correspondence, entertained callers."

Interested people who practiced voluntary poverty helped run breadlines, which fed thousands. "In New York City over a thousand come every morning to breakfast," she wrote. In her diary she also wrote of her deep concern and charity for her neighbors, who were in one of these Houses of Hospitality:

"There are several families with us, destitute families, destitute to an unbelievable extent, and there, too, is nothing to do but to love. What I mean is that there is no chance of rehabilitation, no chance, so far as we see, of changing them; certainly no chance of adjusting them to this abominable world about them."

Dorothy was a very busy lady indeed. While concerned with feeding the people, she had to shelter and clothe them, too. There were essays to be written, the newspaper to be published. There were discussions with many people, countless interruptions, trips to the hospitals, visits with the sick at home, and traveling about the country by bus to establish other houses.

During all of this, her Bible was her constant companion. She also turned to particular saints for inspiration during difficult times: St. Teresa of Ávila, St. Thérèse of Lisieux, St. John of the Cross, St. Francis of Assisi, and St. Catherine of Siena.

Undoubtedly, she drew much from these saints, since those around her often remarked at her forbearance, her stoic endurance, and her ability to kindly tolerate what they considered to be extreme irritations.

While surrounded with the apparent sadness and difficulties of her work, Dorothy's only real joy came from her daughter, Tamara, who stayed with her in various Houses of Hospitality. Dorothy did not feel it was improper for Tamara to witness this unfortunate side of life. She watched caringly and lovingly during her daughter's childhood and teenage years.

When it came time to consider Tamara's higher education, she was sent to school in Canada. In time, Tamara married, and proudly presented the happy Dorothy with a number of grandchildren.

Since Tamara's birth, Dorothy's prayer life had steadily increased. She frequently read and quoted passages from the Bible, her favorite book. She attended Mass every day when not traveling, and said Rosaries while picketing and when her charity work permitted. Above all, she loved the Church and the poor, who were always with her.

Dorothy's ideals were summed up in this passage from her diary:

"What we would like to do is change the world—make it a little simpler for people to feed, clothe, and shelter themselves as God intended them to do. And to a certain extent, by fighting for better conditions, by crying out unceasingly for the rights of the workers, of the poor, of the destitute—the rights of the worthy and the unworthy poor, in other words—we can to a certain extent change the world; we can work for the oasis, the little cell of joy and peace in a harried world."

Due to her inspiration and her belief in man's God-given dignity, there are now two hundred thirty-five Catholic Worker communities in the United States and in the world, which are committed to nonviolence, voluntary poverty, prayer, and hospitality for the homeless, the hungry, the exiled, and the forsaken. Members continue to protest injustice, war, racism, and violence of all forms.

To the day of her death, Dorothy regretted her participation in the sexual revolution of the 1920s, and wrote and preached against the sexual revolution of the 1960s. She wrote in her diary: "This whole crowd goes to extremes in sex and drugs. . . . Also, it is a complete rebellion against authority, natural and supernatural, even against the body and its needs, its natural functions of child bearing."

After having worked almost fifty years in the Catholic Worker Movement, Dorothy—who had become a friend of Thomas Merton and many distinguished writers and churchmen—died with her daughter, Tamara, at her side on November 29, 1980. Dorothy was eighty-three years old. Worn from her labors and the results of a heart attack, Dorothy slipped peacefully into the arms of her Redeemer.

Before her death, it was suggested to her that she might someday be canonized. Dorothy dismissed this suggestion, saying that whatever monies might be expended on this improbability should be spent instead on the poor. However, her call for canonization has received a great impetus, citing her life as one lived in faithfulness to the gospel and to the care of the poor.

Since Dorothy had practiced voluntary poverty since starting her Houses of Hospitality, she left no funds for her funeral. The Archdiocese of New York willingly assumed all costs for a funeral that was impressive. After the funeral Mass, with newsmen and television camera crews moving about the crowd, many of the people who had been helped through Dorothy's efforts milled around. These included Native American, Hispanic workers, African-Americans, and countless American poor.

During the procession from the Nativity Catholic church, Dorothy's grandchildren carried the pine box that held her body. At the church door, Cardinal Terence Cooke met the body to bless it. This was not the first time the cardinal had anything to do with Dorothy. On Dorothy's eightieth birthday, the cardinal's black limousine had driven up to the First Street Hospitality House, and he had gotten out and personally presented Dorothy with birthday greetings from Pope Paul VI.

Dorothy was buried in a cemetery at Richmond, Staten Island, a short distance from the scene of her conversion.

Almost immediately after her death, the question arose as to the propriety of promoting her for the honors of the altar. This was settled a few years later by Cardinal John O'Connor, after consultation with the Vatican. The cardinal then wrote:

"It is with great joy that I announce the approval of the Holy See for the Archdiocese of New York to open the cause for the beatification and canonization of Dorothy Day. With this approval comes the title Servant of God. What a gift to the Church in New York and to the Church Universal." †

Venerable Edel Quinn

⚬∾

1907–1944

Legion of Mary Envoy

IRELAND-AFRICA

$\mathcal{M}$any of the saintly people in this volume performed great works of charity, helping the sick and poor, teaching, and participating in all manner of ministries. But none did so while suffering from tuberculosis as did Edel Quinn, who labored in the Lord's vineyard from the age of twenty-five until her death at the age of thirty-four. During those nine years, despite her illness, she spent herself in the service of others, always joyfully, and constantly with Our Lady as her model.

Edel Mary Quinn was born in Ireland, at Greenane, near Kanturk, a small town in County Cork on September 14, 1907. She was the first child of Charles Quinn, a banking executive, and Louise Burke Browne. Four days after her birth, she was baptized by Fr. Green in the Church of St. Mary at Castlemagner. Her mother meant to name her Adele, with an "e" at the end, but the priest associated her name with the diminutive form of the flower Edelweiss, and so the name Edel somehow stuck.

After relocating a number of times because of her father's employment, her family finally settled in Dublin. By now, the family had grown to include three more girls, Leslie, Mona, and Dorothea, and one boy, Raphael. The children grew in an atmosphere of joy, liberty, and mutual understanding with Edel, the eldest, as the leader.

She was remembered in the primary grades as being, according to the beloved Mother Thomas Aquinas, "a real imp at school, not indeed bold, but always bubbling over with good spirits, full of life and gaiety and up to every kind of prank. She was the center of every group bent on fun or mischief."

There was also another side to the child. "Though carefree and lively, she was never slipshod in her work or her appearance. . . . Her unselfishness and her readiness to do a service were notable. She was a born organizer, and everything she undertook she did well."

For two years, she attended a boarding school in England, where she was remembered as being a highly principled pupil, absolutely reliable, attentive to every duty, kind almost to a fault. Because of her skills, she was chosen as captain of the cricket team, with her other activities being tennis, dancing, and playing the piano.

But her happy days at school came to an end when the family settled in Dublin. It was then that the family's income was decreased, which made it necessary for Edel to contribute to the financial support of the family. Edel was seventeen years old.

Eager to assist the family, Edel attended commercial classes, and upon the completion of her training, she secured a secretarial position at the Chagny Tile Works. Her employer spoke of her as being a model worker and a perfect secretary who quickly mastered and faultlessly carried out all her assignments.

As the eldest child, the family instinctively turned to her for advice, since she held a unique place in the hearts of all its members. In fact, her father's familiar term for her was "Granny," so wise and mature did he consider her recommendations.

All this time, Edel's interior life was progressing to such an extent that a friend who later became a Carthusian nun wrote that she knew Edel Quinn about the year 1930–1931 when Edel was about twenty-three years old. "From the beginning [of our friendship] I felt convinced that I had entered into contact with a chosen soul." The nun continued:

"One sensed about her a consciousness of living in the divine presence. She did not talk about it, but her personality radiated an atmosphere of recollection. Yet she was the soul of gaiety, of cheerfulness.

"That was one of the most extraordinary aspects of her whole conduct: quite naturally and seemingly with perfect ease she combined a deep interior life with all the assets of social success—youth, charm, smartness, love of fun, and innocent merriment, a keen sense of humor, a bright intelligence, a talent for music, and ability at sports such as tennis, dancing, and golf, all of which she loved but later gave up to devote her free time to the Legion of Mary apostolate."

It took her some time to deliberate on her vocation in life, and when she was certain, she made arrangements to enter the Poor Clares of the Colletine Observance in Belfast. Her entry was scheduled for April 1932. She was twenty-five years old.

Her friends were surprised at her decision, but weeks later they were shocked to learn that she had contracted tuberculosis and had been taken to a sanatorium. Some blamed it on her diet, since she fasted, often missing her meals, and abstaining from milk, butter, and meat.

Those who visited her at the sanatorium always found her radiant and full of fun and always able to avoid speaking of the state of her health. She never complained, and she smiled through her pain. She did not stay in the sanatorium for long, however, since she knew her parents, who were not wealthy, were burdened by her expenses.

She returned home and soon realized that all treatments had been unsuccessful. She then decided to direct her attentions and her remaining energies to performing something that was useful. Despite her lingering illness, she found a job as a secretary at a company called Callow's Enginering Works, and she also became a more active member of a Legion of Mary praesidium.

Edel resumed her usual austere existence, fasting and performing mortifications, never permitting her illness to be an obstacle in her pursuit of a closer union with God. The only indulgence she permitted herself was to take a day's rest from work when she experienced a hemorrhage from the lungs.

Her deep love of the Blessed Mother had led her to the Legion of Mary, where her spiritual life flourished. She joined in order to serve Mary better and to bring souls to Christ. Mary was her model, whose virtues and traits of character Edel tried to emulate in her own life.

At this time, she read extensively about the Blessed Mother, especially *True Devotion* and the *Secret of Mary* by St. Louis Marie de Montfort, both staples of the Legion. She was also attracted to St. Thérèse of Lisieux, whose book *Story of a Soul* became one of Edel's most cherished possessions. Among her other favorites were St. Juliana of Norwich, St. John of the Cross, St. Teresa of Ávila, St. Elizabeth of the Trinity, and Elizabeth Leseur, a secular saint of modern times, whose biography follows.

Despite her illness, Edel was always ready to help others. Her weak health was never a pretext for refusing a service. On the contrary, one of the sisters reported that, despite Edel's physical condition, "her most extraordinary quality was perhaps her seemingly unlimited buoyancy. When the opportunity came, she would display an overflowing energy and brightness in her gift of self. For as long as I knew her, I never saw her looking tired or dragging her step. She was always eager to run around helping people."

The only time when those who knew her realized she felt discomfort was when she was seated, since she leaned far back in her chair—a position that apparently relieved her lungs.

Somehow, Edel always seemed energetic. She also displayed a remarkable joy and serenity, even in the most trying circumstances. "Her good humor was unfailing. Moods had no place in her life." She ate sparingly and thought nothing of missing a meal. She retired late at night and, as a penance, slept on a very hard bed.

Because of her tubercular condition, Edel was sometimes accused of endangering those with whom she came in contact. But in Ireland at that time, there was no fear of contracting tuberculosis from a casual association. It was believed that tuberculosis was only contagious if someone slept in the same room with a patient, and that it was only during the last six months or so before death that danger really existed.

When Edel's health improved somewhat, she dreamed of starting groups of the Legion of Mary in England and surrounding areas, and she presented her idea to the Legion. The answer to this appeal came in the form of an invitation for a member to spread the Legion in eastern Africa. She promptly volunteered. Her request was at first contested, but after a meeting of the concilium, the governing body of the Legion, with Frank Duff, the founder, in attendance, Edel's petition was approved.

Now that the family's fortune had improved and the children grown, Edel felt she could be spared, leaving home and her loved ones, knowing that she would probably never see them again.

Following a one-month voyage by sea, she arrived in Nairobi, Kenya, on November 24, 1936, where she secured residence in St. Teresa's Convent. Many difficulties were soon presented. Edel found there were twenty different tribes, most with different languages and dialects who didn't associate with one another. Then there were some Europeans, who also lived apart.

The language barriers were not the only problem. There was the rainy season, which made roads sloppy and inaccessible, so that often Edel had to abandon her driver and her car to walk in the mud to her various meetings. Some journeys were of a considerable distance, which were made extremely uncomfortable, since

Edel had to endure either rain or heat and stifling dust. But despite difficulties, within nine months of her arrival, there were thirty praesidia.

During these hours of travel, Edel spent the time in meditation and prayer, which undoubtedly sustained her, since she overcame all obstacles and established the Legion not only in Nairobi, but also in most of Kenya, Uganda, Nyasaland, and Tanganyika.

Two years after her arrival in Africa, she suffered a severe attack of malaria. But when sufficient strength was restored, she continued her work. Four years after her arrival, she journeyed to the island of Mauritius, where she established on the island thirty branches of the Legion.

Sometime after she returned to the mainland, she suffered a complete collapse, with a return of malaria, and a case of pleurisy that was so bad everyone thought she was dying. This time she was sent for a six months' rest in a sanatorium, where she again continued her activities. If she couldn't leave the bed she could write, continuing her correspondence with the Legion headquarters in Ireland and writing to countless groups in Africa, instructing, encouraging, and supervising activities.

Missionaries saw the good results affected by the Legion: the many who returned to the Church; a large number of converts; a great number of baptisms; those who faithfully attended Mass; and a new fervor in Christian life, which resulted in Edel being besieged with requests for more groups to be introduced. Weak as she was, she continued her work, so that literally hundreds of additional groups were established.

It is amazing that this young woman, suffering from tuberculosis and malaria, could accomplish so much, since at the time she weighed a mere seventy-five to eighty-eight pounds. When one of the sisters saw that she was barely able to walk, yet still undertook widespread visitations by car and train, she said, "If you continue to go about like that, you will be found dead in a car or train someday."

Edel replied, "Our Lady will not allow that." She was doing the Blessed Mother's work, and Mary would assist her, Edel knew, as she continued to establish other praesidia.

After overcoming territorial, tribal, racial, and language difficulties to establish hundreds of praesidia, Edel died on May 12, 1944, at the age of thirty-seven, after touching a crucifix to her lips and pronouncing the name of Jesus. Her grave in Nairobi became a place of pilgrimage, with innumerable favors being attributed to her intercession.

Pope St. John Paul II, in a special assembly, declared: "It is certain that the Servant of God, Edel Mary Quinn, a secular virgin of the Legion of Mary, practiced to a heroic degree the theological and cardinal virtues." With this pronouncement, Edel was awarded the title of Venerable.

Soon after her death, a Nairobi priest declared to a fellow missionary, "Long after we have all disappeared, the name of Edel Quinn will be spoken with veneration on African soil." His words were prophetic, except that her name is now spoken with veneration not just in Africa, but throughout the world. †

Servant of God Elisabeth Leseur

1866–1914

Long-Suffering

F R A N C E

No one can claim that Elisabeth Leseur derived her attraction for religion in her parental home. Her father, a distinguished lawyer at the Paris bar, occupied himself little with religious matters. Her mother, a model of maternal love and care, performed her religious duties without any particular devotion. Elisabeth's brother was likewise cool to religious practices; her sisters, however, were prayerful and pious. Elisabeth's love of the faith was nourished at school, where she received her religious training and made her First Holy Communion in the parish church.

All we know about Elisabeth is found in her biography, written by her husband, who was a confirmed atheist. Felix Leseur was engaged in foreign and colonial politics, as well as being a contributor to important daily papers of the left, or the anti-clerical, party. During the whole of their marriage, he consistently attempted to destroy her religious beliefs, which caused her a great deal of suffering.

In the biography of his wife, which he wrote after her death, we are told nothing else regarding Elisabeth's childhood and maiden years. The biography focuses instead upon the happenings after their meeting in May 1887, in the home of mutual friends. Two years later they were engaged and set about furnishing a beautiful new home. Two months later they were married.

Felix wrote that "she made the home into a center of warmth and gentility, where she frequently entertained friends." He added that, although she was never blessed with children, she loved the young and displayed a maternal love for her niece and nephews.

He also described Elisabeth as a cultivated woman who had learned Latin, English, and Russian and was beginning to master Italian when illness interrupted her studies. Felix was understandably effusive with his rich descriptions of his wife. He wrote that she was very attractive, with mannerisms that were full of distinction and kindness, which made her always smiling and amiable.

Her mind "was open to everything, remarkably quick and penetrating," he wrote. "She rejoiced in everything beautiful in nature or in the genius of man. . . . She knew how to understand and appreciate art in every form—painting, sculpture, music, and literature, and her travels [after her marriage] to Spain, Italy, northern Africa, Greece, the East, Russia, and Germany, had made her tastes very fine and true."

In addition, he wrote, "her conversation was lively, interesting, attractive and spirited, but always simple and modest without ever making a show of her intellectual superiority. She was thoroughly gay and took care to be so always; she even considered gaiety a virtue. . . . Her lovely laughter rang out at every opportunity, with its fresh, frank sound."

This description of Elisabeth's personal and social graces seems remarkable, since she was almost always ill during their marriage and first experienced a health crisis only two months after her wedding, when she developed a painful intestinal abscess that never completely healed.

Felix revealed that he was brought up in a thoroughly Catholic family by parents who devoutly practiced their religion, and that he had been instructed by distinguished priests. During his college years he lost his Christian beliefs and was attracted to paganism and atheism. He even searched for ways to combat Christianity and studied the works of the Catholic Church's adversaries, even going so far as to collect an extensive library of Protestant and rationalist writings.

When he married, he resolved to respect his wife's Catholic faith and always to permit her to practice it freely. Yet instead he systematically attacked her faith, with the ultimate goal of leading her into liberal Protestantism and eventually to radical agnosticism. Because of his persistence, Elisabeth experienced a crisis of faith, and for a time abandoned religion for almost two years.

Felix almost succeeded in his goal. But "Elisabeth, with her unusual intelligence, possessed the even rarer gifts of a sane and steady judgment and uncommon good sense," which brought her back to the love of the Church. After this, she devoted herself to an intense study of the Catholic faith.

Since Felix had an extensive library of anti-Catholic and anti-Christian materials, she counterbalanced it with a library of her own, which included the works of the great masters of Catholic thought: the Fathers of the Church and those exalted writings of the saints, with the writings of St. Teresa of Ávila being among her favorites. Such was her study of these and Scripture that she was able to defend her faith against all assaults.

Elisabeth is said to have been surrounded not only by a disbelieving husband, but also by his friends, who were all men of distinction and learning, but who were also hostile toward religion. After Elisabeth's return to the practice of her faith, when Felix saw that he could not break her strong attachment to her beliefs, he redoubled his use "of criticism, polemics and raillery . . . which caused her so much pain, and this is now the great regret of my existence."

This situation continued until 1903, when Elisabeth was asked to be the godmother of a friend who had converted to Catholicism. It was at this ceremony that Elisabeth met the Dominican priest who was to become her director and spiritual guide. After her death, he confided to Felix, "She was truly a saint."

Elisabeth's whole life was filled with suffering. In her infancy, she suffered from a liver problem that became a perpetual and increasingly painful ailment. During adolescence, an attack of typhoid fever endangered her life. Then, in her adulthood, the intestinal ailment that was to continue to the end of her life began after two months of marriage. This condition required eight months of bed rest, after which she was intermittently able to lead a somewhat normal life.

She later suffered a serious injury during a carriage accident, which placed her life in peril and confined her to bed for two months. During 1907 and 1908, attacks of the liver problem became violent and disquieting, which compelled her to modify her way of life and to reorganize it, since she required rest, spending long hours in an invalid's chair.

It was from this chair that she exercised her greatest influence upon those who visited her. Her room was often the scene of the patient giving to the healthy visitor moral guidance and spiritual direction.

Between her various illnesses, Elisabeth conducted charitable activities. She lavished money, time, and energy on those around her and took naturally to good works, even to founding a place where solitary working girls could live in the nicest and most economical conditions. She also became involved in the popular Catholic Action, which concerned itself with low-income families.

When Elisabeth became too ill to continue visiting the needy, she assumed the duties of secretary, which she performed with exactness until the end of 1913, when her last illness presented itself.

There were other acts of charity, too, which included helping the needy materially and morally.

Elisabeth was said to have had a most delicate understanding of souls and to have shown the greatest respect for their views. She would never allow herself or others to criticize them. She detested harsh judgments, was horrified of malevolent criticism, slander, talebearers, and drawing-room gossip, and she was known to have defended those who were maligned in her presence.

A grave situation developed in 1911, when she was discovered to have a cancerous tumor of the breast, which required surgical intervention. When she recovered in 1912, she and her husband traveled to Lourdes, where she thanked the Blessed Virgin for the success of her operation and for the cure of her sister and young nephew.

Felix wrote that a previous visit to Lourdes had produced in him "a detestable impression." The trip with Elisabeth, however, made a different impression on him. "I returned from Lourdes troubled by what I had seen and felt in that land of miracles."

Unfortunately, painful complications developed as a result of the operation, so that by 1913 she suffered frequently from exhaustion. Except for occasional visits of friends, and now and then a ride in the car, she remained in bed. Felix noted that Elisabeth never complained, but remained smiling in the midst of her worst torments, and even comforted those around her.

Her strength is said to have been derived from the Holy Eucharist, from prayer, and self sacrifice. Often she was heard to say: "Suffering that is accepted and offered up is the best of prayers."

In addition to her physical sufferings, she was to endure great mental distress when her younger sister died, then her father, then her brother's seven-year-old son, Roger, a child she dearly loved. She then suffered the death of her second sister, who was only thirty-two years old, and the dear confidant of her soul. More was to come when Elisabeth experienced the death of some dear friends, the serious illness of her last sister, and her mother's increasingly serious health problems.

Finally, at the beginning of July 1913, she developed her last illness, when widespread cancer was detected. For ten months she suffered atrocious pains, with only brief alleviations. It was to be her Calvary until she died at the age of forty-eight on May 3, 1914.

Her grieving husband wrote after her death that he saw "the look of immortal beauty that she wore upon her deathbed, which produced in me the deepest emotion. Her face, peaceful now after the last suffering, had the calm of another world. One could read beatitude in it, and I sensed—obscurely, because I was still an unbeliever—but in some way with certainty, the truth of the passage in the beautiful Preface to the Mass of the Dead: 'Life is changed, not taken away.'"

Immediately before her death, there was an uninterrupted procession of people who visited at her bedside, giving vent to sincere and touching grief. Although unknown to the grief-stricken husband, they were not only her friends, but also those who had benefited from her charities and kindnesses. The funeral was attended by a great many people, so many, in fact, that the clergy were astonished.

In addition, Felix was informed that many asked, "Who was this woman? We have never seen such a funeral before?"

Afterward, many people to whom Elisabeth had written letters revealed the contents to Felix. It was then that he fully appreciated the beauty of his wife's departed soul. Felix wrote that the letters could be counted by the hundreds, and "are admirable both in form and substance."

It seemed that, in spite of her frequent ailments, she was somehow able to write to people of all walks of life, giving counsel and spiritual advice. She had, in fact, become a director of souls, which her correspondence affirmed. Eventually, Felix was to hear of graces received through her intercession.

Elisabeth's spiritual legacy is found in her *Journal*, which was started on September 11, 1899, during the first illness, when the intestinal abscess that developed two months after her marriage was diagnosed. The *Journal* ended temporarily in 1906, but she had written in a small book, titled *A Book of Resolutions*, which filled in the gap between the ending of the *Journal* until she resumed it in 1911. It continued until 1914, when her last illness claimed her life. There is also a part of her writings entitled *The Daily Thoughts*, which were detached fragments written when her meditations or prayer prompted them.

It should be noted that Elisabeth's *Journal* is not a journal in the true sense, since she wrote irregularly, sometimes with long intervals between each entry. Little has been written about her life, but as Felix recorded, "it is the history of a soul, noting the principal stages of its evolution, a kind of examination of conscience set down by hand at odd moments. . . . Just as her thoughts came to her she put them down, as fast as her pen would write, in a flowing hand, with nothing added later and hardly a word crossed out, showing no sign of effort, but only the impulse of the spirit."

Felix did not know about the *Journal* until after Elisabeth's death, when her sister spoke of it. She revealed to Felix that Elisabeth, in her modesty, had wanted to destroy it, but she had intervened time and again. Finally, Elisabeth agreed to save it, saying, "You are right. When I am dead my dear husband will read this, and it will explain many things to him."

The *Journal*, *Book of Resolutions*, and *The Daily Thoughts* all reveal her renunciation, detachment, voluntary poverty, dislike of the world, sacrifices, acceptance of suffering, abandonment to God's will, and love of God and neighbor.

After reading all that his wife had written, Felix "understood the celestial beauty of her soul, and that she had accepted all her sufferings and offered it—and even offered her very self in sacrifice—chiefly for my conversion." Gradually, Felix's former hostility toward religion gave way to a yearning for Catholicism.

After reading some of the books in Elisabeth's library, he saw the poverty of his former position and realized that he must take the steps toward reconciling with the Church, which he did in 1915.

"Elizabeth had led me to the truth, and in my inmost being I continue to feel her guiding my steps to a more perfect union with God."

He wrote: "I soon had the idea of publishing the *Journal* that, with divine grace, had so powerfully led me. It had become my daily reading; I drew from it so much support, sweetness, and certainty that I told myself it might well be of the same great benefit to other souls as it had been to me." The *Journal* was finally published in French in 1917 and quickly became a phenomenal success when it was translated into all the major European languages.

Not only did Felix reconcile with the Catholic faith, but two years after the publication of Elisabeth's *Journal*, he entered the novitiate of the Dominican order. He was eventually ordained to the priesthood in 1923 at the age of sixty-two. During his novitiate, he was allowed to travel throughout Europe, giving talks about Elisabeth's doctrine and her apostolate.

At the urging of Felix, who was a priest for twenty-seven years, and others, the Church initiated the process for Elisabeth's cause for canonization, which was unfortunately delayed because of World War II. The Church reopened the cause in 1990, which was accepted in 1995. Felix died on February 27, 1950.

Years after Elisabeth's death, Felix wrote these thoughtful words: "Elisabeth, living in the world, fulfilled every duty of her state, and her example shows how it is possible, when one has the will and calls upon divine grace, to live an intense spiritual life and to practice the highest evangelical virtues in the midst of outward activity." †

Venerable Elisabetta Tasca Serena

cx/o

1899–1978

Mother of Twelve

ITALY

𝓜ore than one hundred forty-four testimonials to the sanctity of Elisabetta Tasca Serena were given for her cause of beatification. Written by priests, nuns, and lay people, they give glowing examples of good advice given, of help extended, of good example imitated, consolations received, conversions effected, lessons taught, and numerous examples of those who returned to the practice of the faith because of this holy mother. Hers was a difficult life of raising twelve children amid grueling poverty. In fact, even her life before marriage was difficult.

She was born the last of seven children on April 24, 1899, in an old country house in San Zenone of Ezzelini near Treviso in northern Italy. Near this little village is the shrine of the Madonna of Health, which is also known as the Madonna of the Mountain.

Her parents were Angelo and Luigia Tasca. When Elisabetta was eight years old, her eighteen-year-old sister, Luigia, died. The shock of her death was so traumatic to the mother that she suffered an immediate paralysis of the mouth, which never left her. For this reason, Elisabetta's early formation was given by her father, who was pious, honest, and "full of wisdom."

At the time of her birth, and in the area where she was born, there were two main social groups, the squires and the middle class. The squires owned large tracks of land and great herds of livestock. The middle class worked the land for them. Elisabetta's family lived a long time in the service of these "masters" and "gentlemen of the earth," being poorly paid, so that she and her siblings suffered often from hunger and humiliation.

Elisabetta sometimes called her work the "jobs from tyrants." Often the homes of the workers were unhealthy, and "illiteracy was diffused in serious proportions." For country people at the time, life was one of poverty, sacrifice, austerity, and hard labor, except on Sundays, when they were able to attend Mass in the morning and catechism lessons in the afternoon.

As a child, Elisabetta was vivacious and very active. Sometimes she got in trouble, and at night, "I had to pay for my disobedience." Yet she was also talented in that, when taking the cows to pasture, she brought her crochet hook and made many beautiful things that she sold or gave as gifts. For her parent's bed, she made a whole bedspread and, in addition, made paper flowers and birds that she sold.

Elisabetta was always pious and anxious to spread the Word of God. When she was in her teens, she often brought a group of small boys with her to the pasture. After settling the animals, she assembled the boys under the shade of a chestnut tree and repeated the sermons she had heard.

One of the boys, when grown, related, "I went gladly to the pasture with Elisabetta, because she told me the sacred history and the lives of the saints. One day she told us the life of St. Maria Goretti, and how strongly we must respect the virtue of purity. . . . During my long life, I have always remembered the words of Elisabetta, so much they have been engraved in my heart."

When Elisabetta approached her twentieth year, she began to consider marriage and starting her own family. One young man, Joseph Serena, began to visit her with an offer of marriage, but since she did not love him, she thought it best to consult a priest.

What the priest told her left her uneasy. He said, "Remember that many young men have died in the war, therefore, if you want to start a family, the first one that comes along, take, otherwise you run a risk of being without." Being unhappy with this advice, she visited the sanctuary of the Madonna, where she prayed the Rosary.

At the third joyous mystery, she received an answer to her prayer. "It came to me in the heart a great love, so that when I finished the Rosary, I ran down the hill to his house and told him that I would marry him." At the time of the wedding, Joseph was twenty-nine years old, Elisabetta twenty-two. They were married on April 6, 1921.

On the day of her marriage, Elisabetta wrote, "During the Eucharistic celebration that followed the ceremony, I formulated this prayer: Lord, in the marriage I will always do Your holy will and I accept gladly the children that You will give me; give me at least the grace that some become priests and nuns. Lord, if you want also, take them all to Your service." In time, her prayer was again answered. Of Elisabetta's twelve children, two became priests and two became nuns.

After the wedding ceremony, the newlyweds went on a brief trip to Venice and then took up residence in the house of her in-laws, where she was a joy to the numerous members of the family. "She brought song, sincere and intelligent affection to her husband, and a great Christian culture." And here, in the Serena house, all twelve of her children were born.

Elisabetta described her husband as being "always honest and faithful toward [her], a Christian of great piety, faith, and love, and faithful to his religious duties. He had a horror of sin, was a hard worker and had a great heart toward everybody, above all the poor and the gypsies." Later, however, she was to write, "My husband was a bit hard."

Early in her marriage, she took as her spiritual director Fr. Leopold Mandic (1866–1942), a holy Capuchin who was canonized in 1983. She once wrote: "My Christian marriage was born in the confessional, that of Fr. Leopold, and there this sacrament has had its correct light. That light has brought me to Calvary." For ten years, Fr. Leopold served as her confessor, so that "this woman had the comfort to have the sure word of a saint."

When the children began arriving one after the other, the doctor discovered a serious physical problem. He twice suggested that she might want to abort the baby, or face the serious risk of death. Elisabetta was quick with her response: "Never abortion in my house. If I have to die it is the will of God." And, she added, "My children are my most beautiful flowers, and I thank the Lord that he wanted them to grow in my garden."

Some of her pregnancies were very difficult, with long convalescent periods. It was later written: "In our culture of death, when children are killed before they are born, Mother Elizabetta will be an extraordinary, splendid figure in the Church, a splendid model for those mothers who will want to live in the fullness of the Christian religion inside the sanctuary of their family."

Many years later, when looking upon her twelve children, she was known to have said, "I live in serenity. Those mothers that have killed their children through abortion—how do they live?"

After World War II, Joseph and Elisabetta decided to move to a home of their own. On land owned by a Dr. Maffei, the family of Joseph Serena worked for eighteen years, until November 11, 1963, when Joseph became seriously ill. Elisabetta was to nurse him for six years until his death, and she often had to replace him in the heavy work of the fields. Those eighteen years before his death were filled with the usual difficulties that visit a large family with little money. Many times Elisabetta needed medicine, but was unable to buy it.

During those years, as Elisabetta had always done since her early years, she attended Mass every day, received the sacraments, was involved in parish activities, taught catechism, and sang in the choir. She was devoted to the recitation of the Rosary, to the Stations of the Cross, and to visiting the sanctuary of the Madonna of Health. In spite of her meager possessions, she was generous to her neighbors and often gave of her meager food supply.

She had a great devotion to the crucified Christ and once wrote, "I thank the Lord who gives me the strength to bear my crosses. In my cross I see the Lord who wants me near His crucifix. If in my life I had everything, I would perhaps forget the Lord and be attached to momentary and vain things. God comforts me."

When asked how she was able to clothe so many children in the midst of poverty, she replied that many people gave her clothes that their own children had outgrown. In addition, she served for a brief time as a nanny and made a little money. When the children were older, they bought clothes from the money the family made from gleaning wheat from reaped fields. Also, if the older children wanted some particular article of clothing, they raised and sold rabbits.

Most of the used clothing that was given to them needed repair, which kept Elisabetta's needle very busy. When the children wore the repaired clothing, she told them to "wear it with satisfaction since poverty is not a guilt."

And how did Mama Elisabetta purchase food for her family when she was without money? She paid with commodities from the fields, or with wine, salami, or polenta, which is a thick porridge made with corn flour. She evidently did well in this regard, since all twelve children were very healthy.

When television was introduced to their neighbors, the Serena home did not have a set, nor did Elisabetta desire one. Instead, she made up this little recitation: Channel 1: Go to the first Mass.

Channel 2: Recite the Rosary. Channel 3: Make the stockings and mend the clothes. Channel 4: Work in the stall. Channel 5: Teach the lessons to the children and prepare for school. Channel 6: Prepare the food. Channel 7: Do the laundry, to dry and stretch. Channel 8: Sing with joy. Channel 9: Wish well to everyone. Channel 10: So many jobs to do and never idleness for a moment.

Having only an elementary education, Elisabetta continued her education on her own, studying the writing of St. Teresa of Ávila, St. John of the Cross, St. Paul of the Cross, and St. Thérèse of Lisieux. With her knowledge of Carmelite spirituality, one would think that, if she wanted to join a third order, she would have chosen Carmel. Instead, Elisabetta became a Franciscan tertiary and participated in a course of spiritual exercises in the house of the Sacred Heart at Vicenza. She was an avid reader of the Bible, the Catholic press, and the lives of the saints, including that of her confessor for ten years, St. Leopold Mandic.

When one of her sons entered the seminary, later to become Padre Galileo, she saw the other mothers giving gifts of all sorts to their seminary sons. She took her son aside and said, "Child, we are very poor people. I cannot give you what those mothers have given their children." With tears in her eyes she continued, "Here is your mother's gift, a rosary. With this you will surely reach the altar."

We are fortunate in having seven hundred letters of Elisabetta, and they are said to contain a beautiful calligraphy, a gentle flow of thought, and a deep spirituality. They also display a great familiarity with the Bible and demonstrate a woman of good intelligence, an exceptional memory, and good judgment.

In her golden years, while attending Mass, because of an occasional difficulty with her knees, she frequently had to stand with her hands on the back of a chair. When she recited the Rosary, she spent a long time in meditating on a single mystery, and when she made the Stations of the Cross, she was known to pause solemnly at each station with her eyes half open, her face changing expressions from compassion to pity to pain. Her aspect after receiving the Eucharist was inspiring.

A nun wrote that, as a child, she remembered Elisabetta when she was attending Mass during the harvest season. "As the priest passed, Elisabetta asked if she could receive the holy Eucharist early, since she could not stay for Mass because of the reaping of wheat and the crop of hay. The priest brought her Communion without delay.

"After her thanksgiving, Elisabetta told my mother, 'With Him I have everything. Yes, with Jesus in my heart I have everything and can now go to face my job and the troubles of the day with trust and joy.'"

Another time, the same nun related that Elisabetta told her, "Be always happy. If inside there is something that makes you suffer, don't lose your courage, and remember Him. It will then pass after a prayer, and then sing! If you knew how many sorrows have passed me by with a song. And so it will be for you. And give to everyone one of your smiles."

This, she herself, put into practice. In the few years before her death, she was described as being very afflicted, but she never complained. "She was always happy in spite of her troubles, her physical ailments, and her hard life. And she spread joy."

Elisabetta began her final illness on October 2, 1978, with a lung condition. When she became worse, she was transported with urgency to the hospital of Montecchio, where she remained for one month. All her pains were borne with resignation and without complaint.

For a time, it seemed she had overcome the condition. But on the night of October 23, she was stricken with strong pains in the liver and the intestines which, after diagnosis, required two urgent operations.

After confession, and after receiving the Sacrament of Anointing of the Sick from one of her priestly sons, and in the presence of her children, she died peacefully. She was seventy-nine years old.

The funeral took place on November 5 with twenty-seven priests in attendance. Her parish church in Vo of Brendola could not hold all the mourners. The body of the Servant of God rests in the family vault in the cemetery of Brendola (Vicenza).

Before she died, a priest of her parish of Vo visited her and found several priests already beside her bed. She was calm and serene. The priest wrote, "I have not seen anything similar in my life as a priest. In the face of death that was now imminent, she exclaimed, 'I have done the holy will of God in every moment.'"

Sometime before her death, Elisabetta told her children, "After my death, you will sing for me the *Te Deum* in thankfulness to God for the gifts I have received. Above all, for the fidelity to my Christian life and my twelve children. Eight have been happily married, and especially for the four who became Religious."

Elisabetta once heard someone say that she was afraid of dying. To this she replied, "Not me. I am sure that the Lord will take me in His arms when He sees me. He knows how much I have been afflicted." And this, we believe, is exactly what He did. The Vatican's decree, *Positio Super Virtutibus*, was given in 1994. †

Blessed Eurosia Fabris Barban

1866–1932

Stepmother of Two, Mother of Seven

ITALY

𝒦nown as Rosina, and later as Mama Rosa, Eurosia Fabris Barban lived all her life in small villages near the city of Vicenza in northeastern Italy. Having been born in Quinto Vicentino, she moved with her family when she was very young to Marola, where they maintained a small farm. Rosina's formal education consisted of only two years in the primary grades, since it became necessary for her to help with the work in the fields. Rosina's childhood could be described as a very hard time for a young girl, but she continued her education on her own by studying, above all, the catechism and Bible history.

Always inclined to prayer, she maintained a spiritual life that consisted of devotions to the Holy Spirit, the crucifix, the Holy Eucharist, the Blessed Virgin, and the souls in purgatory. Because of her deep prayer life, as well as her simplicity and innocence, she was regarded as an apostle in the family and in the parish where she taught catechism to young children. Her instructions in religion were also extended to the young girls who came to her house to learn the art of sewing. During this time, Rosina was enrolled in the Third Order of St. Francis.

The death of a neighbor, who was a young mother, changed Rosina's life. The young mother left two babies, one fourteen months old and the other three months old. Living in the house with the two babies were the father, an uncle, and a grandfather, all of whom struggled to care for the babies. For six months, as an act of charity, before going to work in the fields, Rosina visited the house every morning to care for the babies and to clean the house. What deeply distressed her during these visits was the vicious arguing that took place among the three men.

Eventually, it was suggested by her relatives and the parish priest that she marry the father of the two motherless babies. This presented quite a problem for Rosina, since she would be living with three men of different characters who were always at odds with one another. After carefully praying about the matter, and fully realizing the sacrifices she would have to make, she considered the matter the will of God, and consented to the marriage. The parish priest stated at the time that the marriage was an heroic act of charity on Rosina's part.

After her marriage, she became known as Mama Rosa and soon gave birth to seven children of her own. One can only imagine the patience and charity needed to raise a total of nine children in a small house with three quarrelsome men.

Mama Rosa took great care in the religious training of her children, since three of them entered the priesthood and three others, including her adoptive children, embraced the religious life. As would be expected of the husband of such a virtuous woman, he died a peaceful and holy death.

It has been said that Mama Rosa's home was indeed a small domestic church, where she knew how to educate her children in prayer, obedience, the practice of virtue, and self-sacrifice for others. It was also noted that "she sacrificed herself day after day, like a candle on the altar of charity."

Mama Rosa died on January 8, 1932, at the age of sixty-six.

The bishop of Padua, in 1972, initiated the informative process for the beatification of the Servant of God. The Congregation for the Causes of Saints recognized the extraordinary virtues of Mama Rosa when it issued the document *Positio Super Virtutibus* in February 1995. She was declared a Blessed in November 2005. ✝

Servant of God Fiorella Bianchi

❧

1930–1954

Secretary

ITALY

𝓕iorella Bianchi Duca was born in Osimo, Italy, the daughter of Emilio and Maria Duca. She completed her elementary and some of her high school studies, but her education was abruptly terminated by the sickness of her mother. Because of the expenses involved in caring for her, the father found that he could not afford the secretary he needed for his business, so he turned to Fiorella to fill this position. Although working at a full-time position, she continued her education privately and read many books on theology and ascetics.

Eventually, she founded two movements that encouraged prayer, the Center for Christian Girls and the Center for Christian Mothers. The two organizations multiplied into a number of affiliates, which promoted daily Mass, meditation, and adoration before the Holy Eucharist. All her activities were under the careful supervision of the clergy, who held her in the highest esteem. In time, many people were journeying to Osimo to ask for her prayers, her reputation for sanctity having spread throughout the region.

Together with many young people, Fiorella, trusting in the goodness of God, organized a center for food distribution to the poor and the evacuees of the postwar period, which was of great relief to many families.

Fiorella died at Osimo on July 1, 1954. Her reputation of sanctity prompted the bishop of Osimo to declare that she had lived a life of great virtue and open the cause for her beatification. ✝

Venerable Genoveffa De Troia

1887–1949

Victim Soul

ITALY

Genoveffa De Troia was born in Foggia, the city made famous by St. Padre Pio, the stigmatist. Sickness began to visit this humble soul when she was in the elementary grades. Since she was unable to continue due to sickness, it was necessary for her to withdraw from further studies.

As she grew older, she felt called to the religious life and tried unsuccessfully to enter the Institute of St. Anne. She later entered the Third Order of St. Francis. Guided by her spiritual director, the Capuchin priest Fr. Angelico da Sarno, she loved all things pertaining to the Church and worked with diligence to advance in the spiritual life.

During World War II, her confessor established her in a house on Briglia Street to escape the bombardment. But it was necessary for her to move again before she returned to Foggia, in 1945. Upon her return she became gravely ill. The reports of her sickness and her deep spirituality spread throughout the territory, causing many people to "squeeze around her bed" seeking advice, prayers, and inspiration.

Somehow, in spite of her visitors and her intense sufferings, she maintained a huge correspondence with missionaries and those who were unable to visit her. She dictated the letters, which were sent to distant places—giving, so it is reported, great peace, encouragement, and joy. She was especially liberal in giving what she could to the poor and to the parish church and was very interested in the activities of the women of Catholic Action.

Mindful of Our Lord's recommendation to love one another, Genoveffa regarded all the priests she knew, and all the people who visited or contacted her, as "my spiritual family."

She once said that each day she gave attention to the souls that God sent to her, but the night was for Jesus alone, to suffer and pray. In one of her letters, dated 1948, she mentioned what is regarded as her motto: "I pray and I suffer, I suffer and I offer."

Death came to Genoveffa on December 11, 1949, in Foggia, when she was sixty-two. First buried in the local cemetery, her body was later moved to the Church of the Immaculata of the Capucines. The cause for her beatification was accepted in 1970, with her virtues being declared heroic in 1992. At that time she was given the title of Venerable.

Foggia, of course, is the home of St. Padre Pio, to whom Genoveffa was deeply devoted. Several items still kept on a bedside table in Padre Pio's cell include a statue of the Blessed Mother, holy images, and a clock. Next to these is a little biography of Genoveffa De Troia. †

St. Gianna Beretta Molla

1922–1962

Medical Doctor

ITALY

To understand Gianna Beretta Molla, who gave her life for her unborn child, one has to be introduced to the family from which she gained an example of virtue and a thoroughly Christian way of life.

She was born in Magenta, Italy, the second youngest of thirteen children born to Maria and Alberto Beretta, who were extraordinary parents. Both were Third Order Franciscans, who taught their children to live simply, frugally, and with fraternal joy. One of the sons, later a priest, said that they "lived an intense life of piety and evangelical mortification, renouncing even exteriorly all that was superfluous." Both parents attended daily Mass with their children in the nearby parish church. In the evening the Rosary was recited, followed by happy and animated conversation.

The youngest daughter once related: "Never did a strong or uncontrolled word disturb the serenity of the family, never was a reproof from the mother without the support of the father or vice versa; always in accord and always unswervingly, they loved their children and desired to give them a sound and complete formation. The atmosphere of the home was permeated with serenity and peace." There were, of course, occasions when corrections or punishments were necessary, but the offender understood the necessity of it and accepted it as deserving.

In addition to the formation of the children as good and loyal Christians, the parents made certain that each of the children studied a profession, so they could serve the community and work in the professional world in a Christian manner. Their success in this endeavor was evident by the accomplishments of the children.

The eldest daughter, Amalia, died a saintly death while in her mid-twenties. Zita studied pharmacology; Francesco became a civil engineer; Giuseppe studied engineering and became a diocesan priest.

Ferdinando became a respected doctor, as did Enrico, who also studied medicine and then became a Capuchin priest, dedicating himself to the poor in Brazil. Virginia, the youngest, became a doctor and then became a Canossian Sister, working as a missionary in India. The others died during infancy.

Gianna became a doctor, and then a wife, a mother, and a martyr, when a difficult pregnancy required that she preserve the life of the unborn by the sacrifice of her own.

The younger sister, Virginia, who has given a good deal of information about her saintly sister, recalled that Gianna was a normal child who occasionally was punished with her, but who refused to play pranks or get into mischief. Because of the careful training of her parents, Gianna was permitted to receive Holy Communion at the age of five and a half. From then on, Gianna attended daily Mass, even when she was not feeling well.

Gianna was not a brilliant student. She struggled with her studies, especially during the upper elementary grades and high school. Even so, she later completed all the grueling studies necessary to become a medical doctor.

One of her teachers during her early school days recalled that Gianna had a sweet character: "She was always smiling. . . . I never heard a word of annoyance, fatigue or rebellion cross her lips. . . . The fulfillment of her duties at home, in school, in society were for her a sacred duty. . . . Diligent and committed to her studies, she was a model of respect and discipline."

When Gianna was fifteen years old, she suffered the first of her great sorrows when her oldest sister, Amalia, died a holy death at the age of twenty-six. Soon after her death, the family moved to Genoa, where the children could more easily continue their studies. During that spring, Gianna made a retreat, and thereafter began to take her duties and her studies more seriously.

Several resolutions were made, including: "I resolve to do everything for Jesus; every work of mine, every trouble, I offer all to Jesus." "I prefer to die rather than commit a mortal sin." And, "To obey my teacher and study, even though I don't want to, for the love of Jesus."

Gianna had a well-rounded personality. Because of the scenic mountains that surrounded her girlhood home, she enjoyed outdoor activities, which included mountain climbing and skiing. In addition, she was artistic, having painted numerous Madonnas and landscapes, which are still admired and treasured by her family.

She enjoyed playing the piano and attending the theater, opera, and concerts. Like many young ladies, Gianna liked nice clothes, but was always careful to dress modestly, believing that simplicity was becoming to a Christian lady.

However, Gianna had more serious interests. Since she was twelve, she and members of her family had been involved in Catholic Action. Gianna was an enthusiastic member, who was interested not only in advancing her own spiritual life, but also in participating in varied activities that would help children to love God and neighbor and would help the Mystical Body of Christ.

She became a leader, with all her free time devoted to apostolic work. She planned retreats and led field trips for young girls. She planned courses of spiritual exercises and worked untiringly for the good of souls, inspiring many to follow her example. Gianna was to remain active in Catholic Action for more than twenty years.

As a young lady, she visited the poor and sick in their homes and, as a lesson in charity, she often brought the girls of Catholic Action with her. She brought the neglected, disabled, and bedridden food and medicines, and she tidied many a disorderly household.

One particular incident is told of her when she met a friend as she was returning home from tending an old woman. "Please don't keep me long," she pleaded, "I just bathed an old woman and I am now covered with fleas." Even this repulsive situation in the old woman's house did not deter her from her act of charity.

Within a four-and-a-half-month period, Gianna lost both her mother and father. It was then that the Beretta children returned to their home in Magenta after having moved to Bergamo, where it was thought to be safer during World War II.

As to her life's profession, Gianna decided upon a medical career and received her degree in medicine and surgery in 1949 from the University of Pavia. She quickly joined her brother Ferdinando, who was already practicing medicine in Mesero, located not far from the family home. The people of the town flocked to the medical office with great confidence, having known the family's reputation for goodness.

Gianna regarded her profession as a service to both the body and soul of her patients, assisting them free of charge if they were too poor to afford medical help and supplying them with free medicine, supplies, and money. She wrote: "The sick are images of Jesus Christ. . . . The mission of the doctors and nurses is to collaborate with this infinite mercy, helping, forgiving, sacrificing themselves. . . . Blessed are we doctors if we remember that, beyond the bodies, there are immortal souls, which the Gospel urges us to love as ourselves."

Since she was especially attracted to serving mothers and children, she returned to school while still maintaining her medical practice. She received a degree in pediatrics from the University of Milan in 1952.

Gianna was a dedicated doctor who visited her patients in their homes in the countryside, or in the hospital at Magenta. In the afternoons, she spent time in her consultation rooms. She was known not to leave the office until she had served the last patient, sometimes returning home as late as nine o'clock.

Her nurse assistant recalled that Gianna promptly visited the sick at night when they called. One night she was called three times to the bedside of the sick. This round of activities continued until she entered the hospital for the birth of her last child.

Gianna was a serious opponent of abortions. When treating a young, unmarried girl who had aborted her baby, Gianna was horrified. She pleaded with the girl to confess the sin to a priest, and then urged her parish priest to lecture about this unspeakable crime.

She was especially close to expectant mothers, calming their anxieties and happily counseling them up until their time of delivery. The value she placed on life prompted her to write: "The doctor should not meddle. The right of the child to live is equal to the right of the mother's life . . . it is a sin to kill in the womb." This declaration was to present itself later in Gianna's life.

Now settled in her medical practice, Gianna felt called to join her older brother, who was a priest in the missionary field of Brazil, where she hoped to offer her services to the poor, who were so badly in need of medical attention. Because one obstacle after another presented itself, and because she realized that her health was not equal to the Brazilian climate, she heeded the advice of her spiritual director to wait.

Still active in Catholic Action, she often came into contact with a mechanical engineer, Pietro Molla, and it was not long before she knew that he loved her. During the Marian Year of 1954, Gianna accompanied a pilgrimage of sick people to Lourdes, where she prayed to the Blessed Mother for guidance. As she wrote when she returned home, "I reached home . . . and Pietro came in!"

After a seven-month engagement, Pietro, forty-three years old, and Gianna, thirty-three years old, were married by her brother, Fr. Giuseppe, in September 1955. The affection of the people for Gianna was demonstrated at this time by loud clapping while the bride walked up the aisle to the altar, a reaction that surprised and pleased her.

The newlyweds went on an extended honeymoon, touring Rome, Italy, and Europe, and then settled in a little house near the SAFFA Works, where Pietro worked as director. With her usual zest for living, Gianna anticipated a number of children who would bless their union. Before her marriage, Gianna had written to Pietro: "[We will] do all we can to make our new family a little cenacle, where Jesus reigns over all our affections, desires, and actions. . . . We will become God's collaborators in creation."

She continued that she wanted to be the wife he had hoped for and then added, "I want to be [a good wife] because you deserve it and because I love you so much."

After the marriage, Pietro wrote of his happiness with Gianna: "Her holy virtues, the gentle goodness and affection of Gianna, all her cares, give me the full joy and serenity which I asked of Jesus on my wedding day. With Gianna I am sure of forming a truly Christian family on which she will know how to draw the most beautiful heavenly graces."

He added that they would continue the daily recitation of the Rosary, and that they would appeal to the Blessed Mother to watch over them and to give them the grace "to be cheered by little angels." Here were two people of the finest qualities, looking forward to living the ideals of their Catholic wedding vows; a perfect example for every engaged couple.

Three months after the wedding, Gianna conceived, and in due course, in answer to their prayers, their first child, Pier Luigi, was born. Then came Mariolina in 1957 and then, two years later, Lauretta joined the family.

Serious complications developed during each of the pregnancies. With all three she experienced excessive vomiting, intestinal binding, and dysfunction, and other gastric disturbances that caused a great deal of pain. Her first pregnancy went twenty-five days beyond her due date, with a labor that lasted thirty-six hours. The second pregnancy had similar difficulties and was extended ten days beyond the due date, concluding with a long and painful delivery.

During the third pregnancy, she had to be admitted to the hospital due to acute symptoms similar to her first two pregnancies, with vomiting and acute spasmodic contractions, and with the threat of miscarriage. After the symptoms were relieved, she returned home and delivered in due time. According to the attending physicians, the delivery of each child took place without pain relievers of any kind, according to the wishes of the mother.

Despite the difficulties experienced, the births were immediate occasions for thankfulness and joy. Soon after the baptism of each, they were placed under the protection of Our Lady of Good Counsel, and as soon as Gianna recovered from each birth, she continued her medical apostolate in Mesero. Pietro was to write after her death:

"At home you were always busy; I cannot remember you being idle or even resting during the day, unless you were ill. Even with all the work our family gave you, you chose to persevere with your mission as a doctor in Mesero. . . . Your intentions, your actions were always fully consistent with your faith, with the apostolic, charitable spirit you had lived in your youth."

Pietro's engineering profession often obliged him to travel, and on a number of occasions these journeys took him to the United States. During these travels Gianna kept him informed by letter of the children's activities, their progress, and their prayers for the speedy return of their father. As a mother she had many chores in caring for her children, and in spite of domestic help and the help occasionally given by Pietro's mother, Gianna was obliged to omit her daily Mass and Holy Communion, much to her disappointment.

The year before her death, Gianna visited a friend, who was to write: "Gianna enjoyed her children, lived for them and was so proud of them." During the visit, the friend noticed that Gianna "watched the children in silence, and every now and then she arranged the dress of one, caressed the hair of the other and looked attentively at them. One could see that she was satisfied and proud of them. She was so happy."

Gianna and Pietro prayed for yet another child to grace their family, but the next two pregnancies ended in spontaneous miscarriages. In the fall of 1961, Gianna became aware that she was again expecting. The happiness she experienced soon turned into a serious, life-threatening problem when it was discovered during her second month that a painful fibroid tumor had grown in her uterus.

Although a benign tumor, it was rapidly growing and threatening to compress the fetus, which could result in abnormalities in fetal development, if not causing a disruption of the pregnancy itself. Various complications could also result if the tumor remained, including preterm labor and a displacement of the uterus. Additionally, the tumor might outgrow its blood supply and degenerate, causing considerable pain, as well as presenting the risk of infection.

Faced with the diagnosis, Gianna, being a doctor, knew her options. The first was to have a hysterectomy, which would cause the death of the fetus and preclude the possibility of future high-risk pregnancies. The second option would be to have the tumor removed, abort the fetus, but still retain the possibility of future pregnancies.

Gianna could not accept either of these two options, since it would result in the death of the fetus. The third option was to have the tumor removed, continue the pregnancy and leave open the possibility of future pregnancies. Although this third option might present other complications, this is what Gianna decided upon.

Since Gianna was a medical doctor, she understood the risks she was taking: The surgery on the uterus could irritate it to the point that the pregnancy would be threatened and would spontaneously abort. The blood loss could be difficult to control in a pregnant uterus, while such surgery presented the danger that, during the remainder of the pregnancy, there might be a reopening of the scarred wound.

A flare-up of this sort could be dangerous from the rapid bleeding that would result. By accepting this third option, Gianna heroically saved the life of her unborn baby. But in the end it cost the mother her life.

This pregnancy, like the previous three, was met with persistent nausea, complications, and always the threat of a spontaneous miscarriage. Gianna suffered much during her pregnancies, but without complaint. This last pregnancy, however, had difficulties not faced in the previous ones, since a life-threatening situation could develop if the expanding uterus were to press against the ovary, opening the surgical incision.

Gianna remembered a lecture she attended about the duties of a Christian mother and her own counsels to the young girls who participated in Catholic Action. That is, when the mother and child are in danger, the life of the child should take preference. When the options were presented by her physicians, she immediately chose the surgery that would save the life of the baby at a risk to her own.

She was to say, "With faith and hope I am trusting in the Lord even against science's terrible sentence. I trust in God, but now it is up to me to fulfill my duty as a mother. I renew the offering of my life to the Lord. I am ready for anything they will do to me provided my child is saved."

The doctors were later to confess that they had hoped the uterus would naturally abort the fetus, thus saving the life of the mother, but this did not take place. Instead, the surgery went well, and when the fifth month passed, Gianna had hopes that both of them would survive. After a time of recovery, Gianna returned home to her children and her medical profession.

Mariuccia Mainini, who took care of the children while Gianna was hospitalized, remembered the final months of Gianna's pregnancy, in which Gianna lived always calm and in apparent peace. Mariuccia also revealed that the dedicated Gianna attended her patients until the day she was admitted to the hospital for the last time.

Toward the end of the pregnancy, Gianna seemed to have had a premonition of her death. In speaking to her brother, she said, "The greater part has yet to come. You do not understand these things. When the time comes, it will be either he [the baby] or I." And to her husband she said in a firm voice, "If you have to decide between me and the child, do not hesitate. I demand it, the child, save it."

Gianna was admitted to the hospital on Good Friday, 1962. Labor was induced, but contractions were not forthcoming. It was then decided to deliver the baby by cesarean section. Under an ether anesthetic, she delivered a healthy baby girl weighing almost ten pounds. The child was named Gianna Emanuela.

Just a few hours later, Gianna's condition began to decline, with symptoms that included elevated fever, a rapid, weakened pulse, and exhaustion. Then, fully awake and free of the anesthetic, she suffered an intense and overwhelming pain, caused by septic peritonitis, an infection of the lining of the abdomen. This condition was to continue for a week until her death, despite the extensive use of antibiotics.

During this painful abdominal suffering, Gianna declined all narcotic medications because she felt that such drugs did not permit her to be alert. While enduring atrocious pain, she was frequently heard to whisper, "Jesus, I love You. Jesus, I love You!" She had asked for Holy Communion, but due to continuous nausea she was unable to receive. So she pleaded for the Sacred Host at least to be placed on her lips.

All the while she knew she was dying. She once said to her sister, "If you only knew how differently things are judged at the hour of death; how vain certain things appear to which we give such importance in the world."

One week after the delivery, on the Saturday morning of her death, she asked to be taken home. The agony she must have felt at leaving her beloved children, her dear husband, and the infant who needed the nurturing of its mother, must have been overwhelming. She is truly the model of an heroic mother who, for the life of her unborn, sacrificed her own life and gave up for the love of God and her principles all those she loved in this world. Her doctor once exclaimed, "Behold the Catholic mother."

Just a few hours after her arrival home, Gianna died at eight o'clock in the morning, the Saturday after Easter. The date was April 28, 1962. One can only imagine the grief of Pietro, whose wife of only six and half years had left him to a life without her joyous and holy companionship.

Two years later, Pietro was to suffer another tragedy when his oldest daughter, Mariolina, died. Of the other children, Pier Luigi was to enter the business world eventually, marry, and raise a family of his own. Lauretta studied economics. Gianna Emanuela, who had been named for her mother, became a medical doctor like her mother and now cares for Alzheimer patients. She lives with her father in Magenta.

Gianna is buried in Mesero in the new Molla chapel, where her niche is framed in gold.

When Pope St. John Paul II conducted the beatification ceremony of Gianna Beretta Molla on April 24, 1994, during the International Year of the Family, in attendance were Gianna's husband, her surviving children, and four of her sisters and brothers, all of whom, during the Mass of Beatification, received Holy Communion at the hands of the Pope. Later, the Pope met with the family, much to their joy and edification. The feast day of Blessed Gianna was set for April 28, the anniversary of her entrance into heaven.

She was canonized by the same pope on May 16, 2004. It was the first time in Church history that a husband witnessed his wife's canonization.

In honor of this holy mother, a stained-glass window was erected in the chapel of the Newman Center of the University of Toronto on October 31, 1999, the eve of All Saints' Day. Attending the dedication of the window were Pier Luigi Molla and Dr. Gianna Emanuela Molla, the son and daughter of St. Gianna.

This fine example of Catholic motherhood, who sacrificed her life for that of her unborn, could and should be given as an example to all who are contemplating abortion. May St. Gianna help them to choose life. †

Blessed Hildegard Burjan

1883–1933

Founder of *Caritas Socialis*

AUSTRIA

*H*ildegard Burjan was born in Goerlitz of nonpracticing Jewish parents. Little is known of her earliest years, but she was known to have had such a keen intelligence that, at the early age of twenty, she was one of the first women to study philosophy in Zurich.

Here she met the Jewish engineer Alexander Burjan and went with him to Berlin to study political science and economics. Two years later, they were married in the registry office in Berlin. After her marriage she completed her education, receiving her doctorate in philosophy.

One year later, tragedy struck when Hildegard became seriously ill with kidney problems that brought her almost to the point of death. Four serious operations were performed, and several smaller ones, which produced such pain that only morphine gave some minimal relief. For a time, the doctors declared her situation incurable, but apparently the Catholic nuns at the hospital did not, since it was their prayers that helped their patient. One day, the ureter that had caused some of the problems became healthy, the fever left the patient, and she experienced a return to health. Hildegard regarded her pain-free situation as a miracle.

During her six-month stay at the hospital, she observed the selfless and devoted care given the patients by the Catholic sisters and began to learn about the Catholic faith. She was eventually baptized and began a new life, not only, as she said, in the religious sense, but also in the public sense. Already, at the age of twenty-six, she envisioned a life of dedicated public service in cooperation with God's grace.

Because of her husband's business, she moved to Vienna, where she soon became pregnant. Another serious health situation developed when the doctors suggested, because of her delicate kidney condition, that she abort the baby. Her life was once more in danger because of this added strain on her system.

Even so, she refused to submit to an abortion, calling it "murder." She was willing to risk her life for the sake of the child. Trusting in God and in prayer, she eventually gave birth to a healthy daughter, whom she named Lisa.

Vienna at the time was rife with social miseries. Children were endangered, there were unprotected girls, the female workers were exploited since there were no wage checks, and there was no legal protection for them. For these and others, she began a Catholic women's organization known as *Caritas Socialis*, which brought about a tremendous change.

Homes were established for the homeless, the sick were tended, food-distribution centers were opened, and sewing rooms were set up for unemployed women. Hildegard and her first group of ten women started an employment agency, convalescent homes were organized, a hospital for the sick and insane was established, and classes in various skills were started. Also founded were homes for unmarried mothers with children and for homeless girls and women. A system whereby hot meals were delivered to the house-bound and the poor was started. These were but a few of the many services established by Hildegard and her Catholic workers.

Hildegard at this time also became a representative in the Vien-nese Christian-Social Party and served as the first woman on the Viennese local council. In this position, she worked tirelessly for the socially disadvantaged. She was also a member of the national assembly and enjoyed the highest reputation in all parliamentary groups, being regarded as the "conscience of the parliament."

It should be considered that, after her return to health following her near fatal kidney illness when she was twenty-six years old, she continued to experience pain and various kidney difficulties. Yet she continued a monumental amount of work, in addition to main-taining a deep spiritual life. She once said, "We must be completely filled by the insight that we can do nothing at all without grace."

Her motto seems to have been: "Completely for God and com-pletely for mankind." Another might be: "I want to exhaust myself in love for others," and she often advised, "Place all your concerns on God."

The kidney problems for which she suffered most of her life eventually became so severe that they claimed her life when Hilde-gard was fifty years old. Her memory is kept alive by the workers of *Caritas Socialis*, who continue the services Hildegard provided for the needy during her lifetime.

A special tribute was given the organization when Pope St. John Paul II visited Rennweg Hospital in Vienna on June 21, 1998, to deliver words of encouragement to the patients, who were tended with loving care by the members of *Caritas Socialis*.

Hildegard Burjan's cause for canonization was introduced in 1982. Her life was declared one of extraordinary virtue in 1999, and she was beatifed on January 29, 2012. †

Blessed Josefa Naval Girbes

1820–1893

Embroidery Teacher

SPAIN

*T*he simple occupation of embroidery was the vehicle by which Josefa Naval Girbes reached the honors of the altar. Josefa ably demonstrated that the heights of holiness can be reached with prayer, the love of one's neighbor, and the exact performance of duty, no matter how humble it might be.

Josefa was born in the city of Algemesi, located approximately twenty miles south of Valencia, Spain. Her early education was limited to embroidery and the rudiments of reading, but she soon became well informed concerning the doctrines of the Catholic faith.

Known throughout her lifetime as Señora Pepa, or simply Pepa, she received spiritual guidance from her parish priest. These instructions, together with her extraordinary virtues, enabled her to grow deeply in the love of God. By the time she was thirty years old, she was well advanced in the spiritual life, and by the time she was fifty-five she had reached the state of mystical union with God.

When Pepa was still a young woman, she felt called to share with others all that she had learned about her faith. With the approval of the parish priest, she began to teach the art of embroidery to the young women of the town as a means of sharing her faith and fulfilling a ministry she felt certain had been given her by God.

These free lessons were accompanied by spiritual readings and wholesome conversations. Pepa's house continued to become a popular place for young women to practice needlework and to learn the practice of virtue, until it was said that, under Señora Pepa's guidance, her pupils became experts at both.

Her curriculum of study gradually developed from basic catechism to instruction on the highest stages of prayer. She also involved her students in the activities of the parish and, moreover, prepared them for vocations as wives and mothers or as members of religious orders.

Since more room was needed to accommodate Pepa's many pupils, a family friend gave her an orange grove known as the *Huerto de la Torreta*, the "Orchard of the Little Tower." In 1877, many of her pupils began to gather there. Eventually, Pepa's house and the *Huerto* became known as a prenovitiate for Christian mothers.

When Pepa was seventy-one years old, she began to suffer from a heart condition in addition to the other infirmities of her age. Two years later, she peacefully died on February 24, 1893.

Since her spiritual life was shaped by the Discalced Carmelite Order, Pepa's life was marked by a great devotion to Our Lady of Mount Carmel, St. Teresa of Ávila, and St. John of the Cross. Having belonged to the Discalced Carmelite Third Order for many years, Pepa was buried in the Carmelite habit, as she had requested.

This teacher of embroidery and of sanctity was beatified by Pope St. John Paul II on September 25, 1988. †

Servant of God Madeleine Delbrêl

1904–1964

Convert, Writer

FRANCE

$\mathcal{M}$adeleine Delbrêl has been described as having the fortitude of St. Joan of Arc, a sense of mission in the Church like that of the Carmelite St. Thérèse of Lisieux, and an apostolic activity comparable to that of the Servant of God Dorothy Day. While compared to these renowned Catholics, Madeleine grew up in a middle-class French family in Mussidan in southwest France. Her family was definitely not Catholic. In fact, Madeleine described herself at the age of fifteen as "a strict atheist," and felt herself to be in an increasingly ridiculous world. She wrote once: "God is dead. Long live death!"

When her family moved to Paris, she became attracted to the intellectual life of the city and soon attended philosophy lectures at the Sorbonne. Suddenly, at the age of twenty, she experienced a complete conversion. She then wrote: "By reading and reflecting

I found God; but by praying I *believed* that God found me and that He is a living reality and that we can love Him in the same way that we can love a person." She became enthusiastic for the cause of God and maintained this vibrancy for the next forty years of her life.

She arrived in a suburb of Paris, Ivry-sur-Seine, in 1933, which was then a hotbed of communism. She remained in that city for most of her life, laboring for the ordinary people of the streets. Eight years later, she served as a lay adviser to the French bishops' *Mission de France*, a seminary whose main apostolate was to reevangelize the country. She also helped found the Mission of Paris, an effort to form bonds between lay and clerical solidarity with the urban working class.

Madeleine's only desire was to live an unconditional openness to the Gospel and to become a true neighbor to those living near her, whether they were communists or the poor and unemployed. Her intense awareness of God's reality and His presence gave her what was needed in her struggles against injustice in all its forms.

Madeleine was a prolific writer. Her book *The Joy of Believing* continues to inspire many who are struggling each day to live according to the commandments to love both God and neighbor—commandments that Madeleine described as being "inseparable but distinct."

We, the Ordinary People of the Streets was a series of powerful reflections that was published posthumously. In it, she explored the Christian's role in a secular society, the difficulty of faith in an atheistic environment, the importance of the Church, our absolute dependence upon prayer, and the all-important necessity of loving God and our neighbors.

As an award-winning poet, writer, and Catholic layperson, she also founded what is called a gospel community of laywomen dedicated to poverty, chastity, and work among the poor. She published only two books during her lifetime but left a quantity of work that has been collected in four volumes.

Madeleine died at the time of the Second Vatican Council and was deeply impressed with Pope St. John XXIII, calling him an "apostolic genius." Madeleine died at the age of sixty on October 13, 1964, at Ivry. Her meditations on the Gospels have, since 1966, been the inspiration for many in France, Italy, and Germany, with Cardinal Carlo Maria Martini declaring her one of the greatest writers of the twentieth century.

Madeleine's cause for beatification was accepted by the Vatican in 1993.

One of Madeleine's most often remarked phrases was, "I remain dazzled by God." †

Servant of God Maria Aristea Ceccarelli

1883–1971

Difficult Childhood and Marriage

ITALY

*M*aria Aristea Ceccarelli learned to endure disappointments and hardships early in life, beginning almost from the day she was born. She was not welcomed, since the parents had wanted a boy who would later be able to assist the family financially. The parents, Anthony and Nicolina, had sixteen children, Aristea being the twelfth-born. During those days of high infant mortality, only five children survived.

The home was not a happy one; the father was an alcoholic and a blasphemer. The mother worked in their restaurant, but their earnings and savings were used for the father's drinking and gambling habits. Once the father stabbed his wife, making her hide the fact, but she was lame for the rest of her life.

As for the mother, she was always busy in the restaurant and was disinterested in the care of her children, doing only what was absolutely necessary. It was not a happy situation, especially since neither parent showed affection, but only irritation and criticism.

Aristea learned to endure pain for the love of God, beginning with a childhood episode when she was brought to see a physician for an infection under the left eye. When the doctor thought it necessary to incise the area with a hot iron, Aristea watched as everything was being prepared and did not object, but calmly accepted whatever would come. To the doctor's amazement, she kept silent during the procedure and never complained, nor did she make a movement.

Another time, she was brought to the hospital for a scabies condition. Between treatments, she occupied most of her time in helping the other patients. From that time on, she grew more and more in virtue.

When she was six years old, she earned a little money doing errands for neighbors. This she spent on reading lessons given by a girl in the neighborhood. But when the money ran out, the girl refused to continue, exactly when Aristea was beginning to understand the first elements of reading. It was a great disappointment. What education Maria had from that time on she acquired on her own.

The parents apparently found it difficult to support the child, since she was put to work at a tailoring factory when she was only six years old.

She received her first Holy Communion in due course, but when it came time for her confirmation, the selection of a godparent was of utmost concern for the parents. They chose a wealthy lady they knew, who owned a hotel in Loreto. The choice was made in anticipation of an economic return.

At the luncheon after the ceremony, the godmother gave Aristea a gold chain, two bracelets, a pair of earrings, and a doll dressed in the costume of Loreto. All the gifts Aristea received that day she never saw again, much to her disappointment. The father hid them all to sell at a later time. She was also hurt that none of the family attended the ceremony and were indifferent, but Aristea was developing an interior life of her own, being drawn to and loving all things relating to the Church.

When Aristea was about fourteen years old, she was a beautiful girl who caught the eye of Igino Bernacchia, a schoolboy who was one year older. His father owned a shop near the family's restaurant, which Aristea often visited for the needs of the family. Aristea's parents knew of the attraction and thought the match an excellent one for economic reasons.

One day, when Aristea entered her house, she saw a beautiful present waiting for her. Later, Igino's parents came to the house for the official engagement. As she had always done, she consented to this, and immediately thought that this was certainly the will of God.

After a four-year courtship, the marriage took place in the Church of the Crucifix in Ancona. Aristea was then eighteen years old. She entered the marriage entirely unaware of what was to come.

She thought that Igino was a person of trust, who would be her defender and her companion in a loving, religiously oriented marriage. A motto that was to sustain her was this: "If God does not want a thing, there is nothing you can do; but if He wants it, then He will also give me the strength to be able to bear it, and so everything will be all right. After all, what He likes, I also like."

Soon after the wedding, Igino became obsessive and was never pleased with his bride, once telling her, "You have been born for the things of heaven and not for those of the earth." He soon lost interest in her and considered her only a servant. Her in-laws did the same.

The newlyweds had taken residence in the home of Igino's parents, who were, some claimed, not the stuff of saints. They had little regard for the new bride and put her to work in the shop. In the house, she was a maid who tried to perform her work to their satisfaction, but who was often criticized for the smallest incidents.

There were also other problems. Living in the same house was Igino's brother, Lemizio, and his wife, Valeria. The two sisters-in-law could not have been more different. Valeria resented and was irritated by Aristea's prayerful and noble ways and her serene attitude in times of trouble, and she often confronted her about it.

Igino at the same time was developing into an alcoholic, who used abusive and vulgar language to his wife. She, in turn, accepted all in silence and with prayers for his conversion. Aristea was naturally distressed when she learned of Igino's extramarital affairs, which he of course denied. She was once surprised by the husband of a woman Igino was seeing. The man eventually brought the matter to court.

Still another problem presented itself when Aristea developed conjunctivitis only three months after the marriage. The inflammation developed, producing an ulceration and a perforation in the eye. The doctor was unsuccessful in treating the condition, which continued with Aristea enduring sufferings and unbearable headaches. After a nine-day stay in the hospital, she returned to Ancona, where she continued working in the shop despite her bandaged eye.

After five years of treatments and suffering, it was decided to remove the right eye, which was replaced with one of glass. Her doctor, who was Jewish, was struck by her heroic patience and once uttered, "But is this woman a holy stone? of marble?"

Because of the squanderings of the two brothers at the shop, it eventually failed. Aristea continued working until the shop closed and continued to perform her duties as maid in the house. Igino was able to obtain a position with the railroad and was transferred to Rome, eventually leaving in January 1912.

Before leaving, however, the in-laws made Aristea promise that she would return three times each year for seasonal jobs and to help in the house. Aristea saw the will of God in this departure to Rome, finding herself fortunate to be leaving a corrupt and spiritually unhealthy environment—a situation in which she continually practiced the heroic way of patience and obedience.

In Rome things were better, with Igino being faithful to his job and contributing to the household expenses. But he continued to indulge in extramarital adventures. Despite everything, Aristea lived in patient fidelity and incessant prayer. Their marriage, however, was completely dead, with the two of them living as brother and sister.

Aristea delighted in Rome, visiting many of the churches and praying fervently before the tabernacle and statues of the Virgin Mary. She was blessed with a vision of the Blessed Mother with the Child Jesus, and once with St. Joseph also holding the Divine Child Jesus. She also began to consult spiritual directors and to work with those who needed help. She assisted many in their last days, and changed the mind of a woman who threatened suicide.

When Alberto Lucini, a friend of Igino's, died, Igino consented for the widow to live in his house. The trouble was that the woman had a difficult character and an authoritative attitude, which Aristea accepted with patience and affection. Aristea also helped a homeless woman with children, one of whom had typhus. When her brother-in-law also developed typhus, Aristea was the one who cared for him, "so much so that Aristea did everything." Under Aristea's influence, he eventually converted, regularized his marriage, and approached the sacraments.

Conditions at Aristea's home became worse with Igino's rough and impulsive character. He once declared his disappointment in his marriage, which he said he resented from the beginning. Soon he began to abuse his wife physically during the same time he was beginning an extramarital affair in clear and impudent ways with the widow they had welcomed into their home.

Aristea once met with a woman Igino was seeing, so she could ask her to stop their sinful and dangerous behavior. Igino heard of the visit and shamelessly attacked his wife with indecent words and jokes, jeering and humiliating her.

Conditions became so bad that Igino even tried to kill her, threatening her with a revolver. The martyrdom lasted for many years, with more threats of death, only to have someone intervene at the last moment. Aristea consulted her confessor about the matter, who reassured her and gave her helpful advice. Aristea soon began to realize that God, in His goodness, had given her a means of growing in virtue so that she could thereby gain Igino's conversion.

Aristea often visited a church named Corpus Domini, where she began talking to her guardian angel. Once, when she was particularly worried about Igino, she began to wonder if the angels continued to guard the soul while it was in the state of mortal sin. The angel seemed to answer her, "Yes. The angels are saddened by the condition, but we guard them up to their death."

Aristea developed many friends who were exemplary Catholics. Eventually, Aristea became well-known for her spirituality and was often approached by people wanting suggestions and assistance. She also began a friendship with the priests of the Order of St. Camillus de Lellis, who are also known as Camillians. One of them, Padre Giuseppe Bini, became her longtime spiritual director.

Aristea continued her apostolate of caring for anyone who needed help and one day received a great answer to prayer—the conversion of Igino. It happened in a very mysterious fashion. Somehow, he found himself in a church and was approached by a priest, Fr. Don Umberto, who had been a confessor of Aristea for a brief time.

The good priest began talking with Igino, who revealed his life of egoism and vulgarity. In a moment, he was illuminated by the light of grace and changed his life to one of repentance. As a convert, Igino was firm in the faith and practiced prayer, often thanking Aristea for her goodness in spite of the sufferings he imposed on her.

At the end of his life, Igino had to be assisted in everything by his loving and devoted wife, until he died January 30, 1964. At the time, Aristea was eighty-one years old.

When Aristea was eighty-four years old, she developed several illnesses, including one of the lungs, which refused to be healed despite antibiotics. In her weakened condition she could not visit the church, so the Camillian priests often celebrated Mass in her room and even recited evening prayers with her.

On her bed of pain, Aristea once said, "This is my crucifixion," but she never complained and was calm and pleasant with everyone who visited her. She died on December 24, 1971, Christmas Eve. She was eighty-eight years old.

Her funeral was held in the Basilica of St. Camillus de Lellis on December 26. It was the church Aristea had frequented, and where she had left examples of prayer and virtue. Several of the Camillian priests officiated at her funeral service and gave glowing testimonials about her virtue and sanctity. She was entombed in the basilica, where she rests on the left side of the altar of the Sacred Heart.

The last action taken on her cause for beatification was made in 1998. ✝

Servant of God Maria Carolina Scampone

1877–1951

Mother, Widow, Indigent

ITALY

$\mathcal{M}$aria Carolina Scampone was the wife of a difficult husband, a mother of five, a widow, a Carmelite tertiary, even a prisoner during World War II. In the end she was an indigent woman, who died in a Roman hospice for the aged poor. She attained holiness and the attention of the Church by living a difficult existence in a spirit of confidence in God and by taking advantage of the difficulties of daily living to offer all to God in a spirit of love. As a simple, devout woman, Carolina recognized the Cross as the source of grace and spiritual growth.

We learn that Carolina came from a devout family and was born the first of four children in Esperia Inferiore, a town situated between Rome and Naples. Later, because of the father's work, the family relocated to Selvacava.

The Mancinelli family participated in devotions closely related to the liturgical year. Lent was a time of fasting and penance. On Holy Thursday and Good Friday, the single meal consisted of bread and beans.

On Holy Saturday, nothing was drunk until the paschal bells had pealed. On Easter Sunday, after the father blessed the bread and eggs for breakfast, Carolina, as the eldest child, knelt to ask her parents' forgiveness for whatever naughtiness she had committed during the previous year.

Christmas, too, was observed with appropriate devotions. These practices Carolina later instilled in her own family.

As an early indication of her virtue, the following example is given. One Christmas, Carolina, who possessed a very pleasant voice, had joined in the singing of a hymn, when a girl who was known to have been jealous of her kept kicking her in the leg. Later, when a friend told her she should have given the tormentor a good slap, Carolina replied:

"That's not the way to earn merit. We should always do good and flee evil, and the Lord will reward us in eternal life, even if there is no hope of being understood here and now. Here we are living in a place of exile, on the terrain of trial for eternal happiness." This spirit is said to have animated Carolina's entire life.

According to the custom of the time, when Carolina's father, Felice Mancinelli, decided that Carolina was the proper age to be married, he selected for her a young man, Rocco Antonio Scampone, one of his employees. It was hoped that Rocco would help to maintain the business the father had started. At first Carolina declined, but in obedience to her father she consented to the marriage, which took place in the parish church of Selvacava.

Rocco was not a devout man, but after he and his bride moved into her family's home, he participated in the family Rosary and watched with interest during the catechetical instructions given for neighborhood children.

In time, Rocco proved to be nervous and irritable, with a fierce temper. Carolina suffered greatly from his abuse, but being patient and long-suffering, somehow she was able to hide her troubles from her parents.

A daughter was born two years after the marriage, but Rocco was displeased and showed disdain for his daughter, who was named Erminia. However, when a son, Felice, was born, Rocco accepted the child eagerly and with great affection. To his delight, two more sons followed, Benedetto and Placido.

After the birth of this last child, Rocco was found to have cancer and was bedridden for the most part between the years 1909 and 1911. Carolina served her ailing husband with love and patience during these difficult years and thanked God most profoundly when Rocco asked for the sacraments of the Church before he died. After his death another son, Rocco Antonio, was born.

After her husband's death, the needs of the widow's family were met by her parents, but this comfortable situation did not last long. Carolina's mother died shortly thereafter, and her two sisters left home—one to be married, the other to travel to the United States. Then, when Erminia was ten, Carolina's father was forced to stop working due to illness and old age.

It was then that the family sank into poverty. Carolina's brother, Felice, did what he could to help. But in 1919 he suffered a paralyzing stroke, received the sacraments, and died.

Left with five small children, Carolina, for the first time in her life, went looking for work. During the winter she joined the olive pickers, and with her meager earnings she was able to bake bread for the family. In the summer, Carolina spent her days in the hills gathering wood, which she sold each evening. During these difficult times, her neighbors noticed that her chief characteristic was patience.

One of these neighbors, Maria Civita, recalled: "She was poor, but she gave whatever she had to those who knocked at her door, depriving herself in the process. . . . She was counselor and teacher to the people of our town. Yet, frequently, I saw her in tears, recommending herself to Providence because she did not have enough bread to provide for her ailing father and her children."

Erminia, who had been caring for her younger brothers, one day anounced that she had a religious vocation and entered the Sisters of the Poor of St. Catherine in Siena. Carolina welcomed her daughter's vocation, but had mixed emotions at losing her company and help.

Carolina's sons took different paths. Felice, when he was only fifteen, joined the Carabinieri, the Italian national police force. An intelligent young man, he was soon earning enough to relieve his mother's difficulties, but this would end abruptly.

One day, while at home on furlough, some friends were testing his service rifle. Just as he warned them that it was loaded, the gun went off, hitting Felice in the stomach. Although he was rushed to the hospital, he died hours later. The shock of this accident caused Carolina to suffer an epileptic seizure, a disorder that was to plague her the rest of her life.

Once again, Carolina had no means of support and was forced to engage in several menial jobs. But another affliction was to visit her in the form of an inflammation of her left eye. There were visits to the doctor, but she was treated only as long as she could pay for his services. She then became resigned to losing her sight in that eye. During this ordeal, her children remembered her as being resigned to her suffering, and she was heard making frequent ejaculations as she went about her work.

Carolina's heart was greatly afflicted by the paths in life taken by her three remaining sons. When a cousin emigrated to Argentina, thirteen-year-old Placido went with him. Since he neglected to write, Carolina lost track of him for many years.

Benedetto, at twenty-one, was drafted into the army. Rocco, a sickly youth, could do little to help, but his beautiful tenor voice attracted the attention of traveling artists, who enticed him to join them. Despite his mother's wishes he left home, only to be arrested with many others when the hotel in which they were staying experienced a theft.

With the European code at the time being "guilty until proven innocent," Rocco spent two years in prison. All this time the mother grieved, thinking her son was dead. But when he returned home after two year's imprisonment, she was overjoyed.

Carolina's happiness knew no bounds when Rocco began serving Mass once again and showed signs of a religious vocation. He entered the Company of St. Paul, where he worked in the printing shop. This, however, was not to last, since a serious arthritic condition caused his superiors to send him home. He continued to live a religiously oriented life and died in June 1936.

With one son in Argentina, another in the army, and her only daughter a Religious in Siena, Carolina was alone. But she never deviated from her religious observances or from helping those in need. She also continued to experience epileptic attacks.

More troubles awaited Carolina when World War II erupted and the German forces requisitioned all they could find in her village. This did not, however, satisfy the Germans. Many of the villagers, including Carolina, were forced to accompany them as they retreated.

One of the neighbors, Giuseppe de Bellis, described the situation: "With my family and Carolina, I left home and belongings with great sorrow. With the Germans we found ourselves at the front. . . . We lived in caves on the mountain (of Monte Casino), and the rumble of the bombardment deafened us.

"In all this desolation, Carolina was our comfort. Still impressed on my mind is her image: comforting us, advising us not to lose courage because the Lord would help and support us with His grace. . . . I could not understand how she could be so calm because we were overcome with fright."

Carolina's sister, Lucia, also remembered some details of Carolina's sufferings: "When the Germans invaded Selvacava, they took the poor thing [Carolina] from the Mancinelli house and carried her off. Carolina was sick and did not have the strength to follow; she fell several times, but the retreating soldiers made her get up. There was no time to lose!"

Eventually, Carolina, hungry and sick, was imprisoned and sent to a concentration camp where her daughter, Sr. Erminia, was permitted to visit her. During the final months of the war, Carolina suffered not only from her epileptic attacks, but also from a rash that caused a high fever and great discomfort. Later removed to the well-known *Santo Spirito* hospital near the Vatican, Carolina endured two painful operations, which forced her to remain two years in the ward for the chronically ill.

Since the hospital was overcrowded, sometimes a meal was forgotten or other inconveniences were experienced. But Carolina never complained, and she regarded these difficulties as opportunities for spiritual growth.

Carolina was eventually transferred to the Institute Santa Maria della Providenza in Rome, where she spent six years. Her nurse, Sr. Maria Barca, remembered:

"In 1944, 1 had the honor of welcoming Maria Carolina Scampone into our house of *Santa Maria della Noceta*. She was very good; she spoke little, but her face was absorbed in prayer. During her long suffering there was never a word of complaint. She was the best in the ward. I recognized her as a soul of outstanding virtue."

Carolina was able to follow the daily schedule of the sisters and received Holy Communion every day. She was even able, at times, to help her sick companions.

During the Holy Year of 1950, Carolina had the joy of having both Sr. Erminia and Benedetto in Rome to gain the indulgence. She considered herself honored to visit the four major basilicas with them. Then, just before Christmas, Carolina suffered a stroke that paralyzed her left side. Sr. Erminia heard her mother constantly praying and saw to it that her mother's longstanding desire to become a Carmelite tertiary was realized.

The chaplain of the hospital, Fr. Giovanni Marini, testified: "The undersigned chaplain . . . attests that he often attended Mrs. Carolina Scampone, a patient in the institute, and found her a wholly dedicated soul. She was all for God, completely resigned to the will of God. She was a model of patience in bearing her afflictions.

"She died in the infirmary of the institute on February 5, 1951, with all religious consolations. Some days before her death she wished to become a member of the Carmelite Third Order and to be enrolled in the Scapular of Our Lady of Mount Carmel. The undersigned, with faculties obtained from Fr. Ignatius of the parish of San Pancrazio, enrolled this holy woman in the Third Order and in the Scapular of Carmel."

Caroline died after a five-day agony and was buried in Rome's *Campo Verano* cemetery. Since that time, her life's story has become widely known, with favors of all sorts being reported as a result of her intercession.

Carolina's biographer noted: "Above all, Mama Carolina is proof, if any is needed, that authentic Catholic holiness is to be found in the concrete and simple ups and downs of our personal earthly pilgrimage." Carolina is a grand example to mothers that all difficulties—the abuse of a husband, the heartbreak of the loss or separation from children, a loss of security, hard menial work, and painful illnesses—can be used for our benefit by offering all to God in a loving spirit of confidence in Divine Providence. †

Venerable Maria Chiara Magro

1923–1969

Teacher, Longtime Sufferer

ITALY

Maria Chiara Magro attained sanctity through her work with Catholic Action in her parish and diocese. She served for many years in this organization, performing all sorts of charitable deeds in its many apostolates. On the diocesan level, she became an executive of the organization; on the national level, a promoter. Her principal activity was teaching on the elementary level for many years and also teaching in the group known as *Boccadifalco*, in Palermo, the city of her birth.

If her family had permitted, she would have entered a cloister. But under the guidance of her spiritual director, she chose to devote herself to the Lord by remaining in the world. She was welcomed into the Institute of the Missionaries of the Work of the Royalty in 1947, an affiliation that allowed her to deepen her spirituality in the Franciscan spirit of humility and simplicity.

When Maria was thirty-six years old, her doctors discovered an incurable ailment. It produced a long ordeal of suffering, with the necessity of several surgical interventions.

She accepted her condition in a gentle manner, offering her sufferings in union with those of Our Lord for the welfare of priests. Her ordeal lasted ten years, but during the whole time, she radiated a spiritual charm that impressed and inspired many.

Maria died in Rome on December 9, 1969, at the age of forty-six. She was declared Venerable in 1995. †

Blessed Maria Corsini Quattrocchi

❦

1884–1965

Professor, Writer

Italy

$\mathcal{A}$ long-held desire of Pope St. John Paul II was realized on October 21, 2001, when for the first time a married couple was beatified together. The date of the ceremony had been carefully chosen, since it coincided with the twentieth anniversary of the publication of *Familiaris Consortio* (On the role of the Christian family in the modern world). This beatification fulfilled the Pope's desire to offer the world a modern example of sanctity in marriage.

The wife and mother of this extraordinary team is Maria Corsini, who was born in Florence to Julia Salvi and Angiolo Corsini, a captain of the grenadiers in the Royal Army. Because of the father's frequent military transfers, the family moved to Pistoia, Arezzo, and finally to Rome. There Maria attended school and received the early sacraments.

Her parents made certain she received a thorough education through the instructions of the parish priests and especially in literature with "teachers of notable cultural levels." Her education in literature was to serve her later in life when she became a professor and began a writing career, which produced a number of essays and books about education, religion, the family, and the spiritual formation of children. Being highly educated, she also became a lecturer.

During her years of study she met her future husband, Luigi Quattrocchi, through the friendship of the two families. Luigi was born in Catania, January 12, 1880. When he came of age, he began the study of law and was named an honorary magistrate in August 1905. He later became the honorary deputy attorney general of the Italian state and served on the boards of various banks.

Maria and Luigi shared intellectual and artistic interests, and by March 15, 1905, they became engaged. Maria at the time was twenty-one years old; Luigi was twenty-five. Their marriage took place in the magnificent basilica of St. Mary Major in Rome. The newlyweds lived with Maria's family in marital bliss and in the love of God, and in time enriched the family with the addition of four children.

The firstborn was Filippo, who became Fr. Tarcisio, a diocesan priest in Rome. The second was Stefania, who became Mother Cecilia of the Benedictine Order in Milan. She served her community as superior for eighteen years and died in 1993. The third child was Cesare, who became Fr. Paolino, a Trappist, and lived in monastic life for more than seventy years.

The fourth born was Enrichetta. The birth of this child presented critical problems, so that the obstetrician suggested an abortion to save the life of the mother. Maria protested. Placing her trust in God, she brought the child to term during the difficult pregnancy and lived another fifty-one years. Enrichetta much later explained that the possibility for survival of a mother in Maria's condition was about five percent.

The children, as can be imagined, were nourished in a truly Catholic family under the wise counsel of a Franciscan priest. They attended Mass and received Communion every morning, and they recited morning prayers together, as well as before meals and in the evenings. The day inevitably ended with the recitation of the Rosary and an examination of conscience.

In addition, the family was consecrated to the Sacred Heart of Jesus, with a picture solemnly displayed. Each year, the consecration was renewed. First Fridays were observed each month, as well as periodic Eucharistic adoration.

Both parents were guided by the same spiritual father, a member of the Franciscan Order, and it is not surprising that when they decided to join a Third Order, they chose that of the Franciscans. Maria, for a time, was also under the direction of the Dominican Padre Garrigou Lagrange, the great teacher of mystical and ascetical theology. With the consent of their spiritual director, Maria and Luigi pronounced the "difficult vow of the most perfect," which is the renouncing of marital relations. This vow was taken after twenty years of marriage when Luigi was forty-six and Maria forty-one.

In addition to their many educational pursuits and the raising of a family, both parents were engaged in a number of apostolic activities, since they were both members of several religious associations. During World War II, Maria volunteered as a nurse with the Red Cross and worked with Luigi as a helper for the sick, who were being taken by train to Lourdes and Loreto. Maria also helped the Church as a catechist for the women of the parish of St. Vitale and belonged to the women's division of Catholic Action, participating in many other activities for the Church.

Maria, with Armida Barelli, whose biography is given in this book, also helped many students to attain an education at the Catholic University of the Sacred Heart. Not only did Maria and Luigi work at various apostolates outside the family, but the Quattrocchi home was always open to the most cordial and cheerful hospitality during the war as a haven for refugees and for those who turned to the couple for comfort or help.

Enrichetta, the youngest daughter, now cares for her brother, Filippo (Don Tarcisio). She stressed that love existed at home. "It is obvious to think that at times they had differences of opinion, but we, their children, were never exposed to these. . . . They solved their problems between themselves, through conversation, so that once they came to an agreement, the atmosphere continued to be serene."

The surviving children also recalled that their family life was never dull, since there was always time for sports and holidays at the mountains and the sea. And there was also an involvement with a scouting group, organized by their parents for the youths of the poor sections of Rome.

During this time, Luigi continued work and became a personal friend of many politicians, including Alcide de Gasperi and Luigi Gedda, who worked for Italy's rebirth after World War II. Both these friends are Servants of God awaiting beatification.

For more than forty years this outstanding couple lived an ideal Christian life, so that the prefect of the Congregation for the Causes of Saints, Cardinal Jose Saraiva Martins, said of them, "They made their family an authentic domestic church, open to life, prayer, witness of the gospel, the social apostolate, solidarity with the poor, and friendship. . . . Intimately united in love and Christian ideals, they walked together on the path of holiness."

Luigi died at the age of seventy-one of a heart attack, leaving his wife to live in her widowhood for fourteen years. She died in 1965 at the age of eighty-one.

Because they had been involved in several forms of marriage and family apostolates, organized in their memory was the *Foundation Luigi and Maria Beltrame Quattrocchi*. Its goal is to prepare couples for marriage and to help the married to deepen matrimonial life.

A ceremony that promulgated the decrees of their heroic virtues was attended by their three surviving children on July 8, 2001. A miracle gained through their intercession was approved, clearing the way for their beatification, which took place on October 21, 2001. The two Quattrocchi sons concelebrated the beatification Mass with the Pope. Afterward, still in their liturgical garments, Fr. Tarcisio (Filippo), age ninety-five, Fr. Paolino (Cesare), age ninety-one, and their sister, Enrichetta, now in her eighties, were privileged to meet privately with the Pope.

Seven days after the beatification ceremony, the relics of Blessed Luigi and Maria were transferred to a crypt in the Shrine of Divine Love in Rome. †

Servant of God Maria de la Luz Camacho

1907–1934

Martyr

MEXICO

Imagine a small group of women led by an attractive lady of twenty-seven standing by the front doors of a church, guarding it against sixty angry and intoxicated men who were bent on burning the church to the ground. Maria de la Luz was not only guarding the church, but the children inside who were attending Mass.

Hoping to detain the ruffians, who were shouting, "God is dead!" or "There is no God!" Maria de la Luz hoped the children and the priest would be able to escape from a back door before the men barged into the church to accomplish their mission. The women were determined, and each time the hoodlums shouted a blasphemy, Maria de La Luz and her group shouted in response, *"Viva Cristo Rey!"* ("Long live Christ the King!"), the cry of the resisters who were defending their faith against a government that meant to destroy it.

Annoyed by the delay and no doubt humiliated somewhat in being thwarted by a group of women, they ended the standoff by shooting Maria de la Luz and the others. The men soon became frightened on seeing the dead women covered with blood, who had been so valiant in defending their Church.

The Red Shirts, as they were called, finally fled from the scene. The children and the priest with the sacred Species had already left the church in safety.

This brave young woman who had died for her faith was born in Mexico City on May 17, 1907. She was named Maria de la Luz, "Maria of the Light," a name known throughout Mexico for the Blessed Mother. She was the daughter of Manuel Camacho, a businessman. Her mother, Teresa Gonzales, died when Maria was only a few months old.

Whereas Maria was a loving child, she was also given to tantrums and had a stubborn nature. Terrible temper tantrums often exploded during her early years, but she always asked for forgiveness. After a time her father remarried, and soon Maria had a younger brother and sister.

When this stepmother died, the family accepted the hospitality of the maternal grandmother and aunt. After a few years, Maria's father married this aunt, who was strong in the Catholic faith and provided a happy and loving home.

Maria had been born during a time of relative peace, but then came waves of persecution against Catholics. Laws were passed in Mexico in an effort to suppress the faith. Churches and convents were turned into barracks, and priests were hunted and imprisoned.

Other churches were eventually closed in protest, with homes being turned into sanctuaries for the Blessed Sacrament and for the secret offering of Mass. Priests who were not arrested wore disguises as they went about ministering to the people. Catholic Action was strong, and Maria became caught up in the wave of patriotism and love of God.

Since priests were few, people were trained as catechists, including Maria, who was just fifteen. Every Saturday night, she instructed about eighty children in her home. She kept notes of her conferences and instructions, which were based on a well-balanced doctrine of virtue and prayer.

When not preparing her lessons for the children, Maria was a great help around the house, cleaning, gardening, and repairing things. She loved music and played the violin. She was also a lighthearted person, who often sang as she went about her chores. She also had an outgoing personality and was often impetuous and high-spirited.

However, she suffered somewhat because of unkind remarks made by jealous people, and though she suffered interior trials and scruples, she never complained. She once told her spiritual director, "I do good and I let people talk. . . . When one can bear the pain alone, why make others suffer?"

Maria also liked to act, and as a child she had writen plays in which her brother and sister had performed. Now that she was older, she wanted to put her talents at the service of God, so she wrote and presented plays for the people of Coyoacan.

There were a number of chances for Maria to accept marriage proposals. But she rejected them all, telling her friends that anyone contemplating marriage should consider the responsibilities entailed in such a vocation. Instead of marriage, she contemplated a vocation to the cloistered Capuchin order.

When she was twenty-five years old, she wrote to her father: "I will work at some employment, but I would not like to impose the expense of a dowry on you. The ideal I have forged for myself is one of sacrificing myself for God our Savior."

She knew well what the religious life entailed, once writing that it was "an anvil on which God hammers His saints into shape with the hammer of sacrifice." She decided to stay home for a time, helping in the home and earning money for the dowry that was needed for her entrance into the convent.

Maria joined the Third Order of St. Francis in 1930 and worked tirelessly in collecting clothes and funds for the poor. She worked among the very poorest and destitute of the city, teaching catechism to the children and adults, in addition to teaching them to read.

When persecution against the Church flared in 1932, churches were set on fire. In one of these, two religious were burned to death. Catholics lived in fear once again.

A friend once asked Maria, "What would you do if you had to choose between losing your faith to be happy in this world, or living in the other world by dying to preserve your faith?"

Maria answered, "God would give me the grace to be faithful to Him. Besides, if I had the misfortune to deny my God, I should die of grief."

When the anti-Catholic Red Syndicate held a meeting in the park across from the church at 10 o'clock in the morning of December 30, fifty or sixty youths in their red and black uniforms gathered to plan the burning of the parish church of Coyoacan. To bolster their courage, they began drinking cognac. When Marie heard of their plan, she went home and put on her best dress.

When asked why she was dressing so carefully, she responded, "We are going to defend Christ, our King." Then she and her sister left their loving home to defend the church and their faith.

On reaching the church, they stood bravely before the front doors. When the Red Shirts taunted them and said it was not good to be Catholic, and that the Catholics would see terrible things, Maria responded, "We are not afraid. If it becomes necessary, we are ready to die for Christ the King. Those who wish to enter this church must first pass over my body."

About twenty people, upon seeing the two sisters standing so valiantly at the church entrance, joined them. Among them were mothers holding the hands of their children, young women, and workers. To the taunts of the soldiers they shouted back, "Long live Christ the King! Long live the Virgin of Guadalupe!"

This was met with "Long live the Revolution!" The Red Shirts began shooting as they charged forward. Maria was shot in the chest and died quickly.

After the usual autopsy, the body was returned to her father's house. That night, more than two thousand people visited the young martyr, pressing rosaries and religious objects to her body. During the night a priest came with palms, which he placed beside the body. He admonished those who were crying:

"There is nothing to cry about. It is not death which has entered this house, but rather a blessing from heaven. . . . We do not need to pray for a martyr. Rather, it is she who must pray for us. . . . Maria de la Luz, virgin and martyr, pray for us . . . pray for our beloved Mexico."

The death of this young martyr was reported in newspapers throughout the country. Telegrams of protest were sent to the president of the republic, which provoked many protests against the radical groups.

People who had read the newspaper reports journeyed to Coyoacan for the funeral and lined the streets from the Camacho home to the municipal cemetery of Xoco. Then a procession began, with a hundred children dressed in white carrying palms. They were followed by a group of young women also dressed in white, and by young men who belonged to a group of resisters. It is estimated that thirty thousand people escorted the young martyr to her grave as they sang and prayed.

Even the archbishop of Mexico, D. Pascual Diaz Barreto, joined the procession. He was overcome with emotion on seeing the thirty thousand people who came without fear of the government, to render homage to an heroic young woman who gave her life for Christ.

Maria de la Luz Camacho's cause for beatification was announced on December 13, 1992. †

Venerable Maria Gioia

1904–1931

Founder of a Lay Association

ITALY

𝓜aria Gioia's parents were financially secure and were so religious that they were clearly distinguished from the other families in the village of St. Elpidio a Mare, where Maria was born. Her devout parents taught Maria her first prayers, introduced her to the love of God, and saw to it that she received her first Holy Communion before she was six years old. Unfortunately, soon afterward, her mother died, leaving her early spiritual development to the care of the father.

During her adolescence, she became interested in working for the Church. She later founded a flourishing association of aspirants and young people who developed a spirit of sacrifice and were dedicated to their spiritual formation. Because of her poor health, she could not work with the group as she had hoped. But she was not far from them, always writing letters of exhortation and encouragement. She was especially dedicated to performing penances for the return of young people who had strayed from the Faith.

When she was able, she lovingly took care of the local church by cleaning and adorning it with flowers. Feeling that her health had improved, she applied for admittance into the order of Dominicans. There were times when she felt encouraged, but then there were times of disappointment. It seemed the good Lord wanted her united with Him in His sorrows, since she was not accepted because of her poor health.

When she was twenty-four years old, she experienced the first symptoms of pulmonary tuberculosis. It was recommended by her physicians that she leave the area for a more suitable climate, but this change did not show an improvement.

She suggested to her spiritual director that she be permitted to make a vow of virginity, which the priest permitted her to make on September 12, 1930. At Christmastime of the same year, she was permitted to make a vow to act in all things in the most perfect manner.

Maria died on March 7, 1930, at the age of twenty-seven, with a reputation of great sanctity. She was declared Venerable by Pope St. John Paul II on April 6, 1998. †

Servant of God Maria Marchetta

1939–1966

Victim Soul

Italy

St. Augustine once stated that pain alone does not make one a martyr; it is the motivation and the spirit for which one suffers that gives the merit of martyrdom and holiness. In the lifetime of Maria Marchetta, we find this motivation and a brave spirit that prevailed during her fourteen years of suffering.

She was born in Grassano in the Diocese of Tricarico on February 16, 1939. Her parents, Domenico and Filomena Bonelli Marchetta, moved to this agricultural area and in time had a family that consisted of Maria and five sons. Maria was the firstborn.

A Franciscan spirituality permeated the house. It coincided with the simplicity of the family's living conditions and its spirit of prayer. Influenced, no doubt, by her active and rowdy brothers, Maria gave free vent to her vivacious character.

She quieted somewhat during her adolescence and passed her time between school, family, neighbors, and her work in the charitable activities of Catholic Action. During her middle school years, she attended the School of St. Clare in Tricarico, but stayed only a few months, when she began to have strange pains in her legs. This problem continued during the vacation break in the school year of 1951.

When she was only thirteen, in January 1952, Maria returned to school, but the situation only grew worse. Every movement was painful and accompanied with a weakness that confined her to bed. It was impossible for her to finish her studies. She returned to Grassano with the hope that her health would return and that eventually she would be able to return to school.

Unfortunately, her condition only grew worse. Various doctors were consulted, but the only diagnosis was some kind of rheumatic crisis. The condition developed to such a degree that Maria had to remain prone on a flat bed. Any movement was desperately painful.

The frantic parents tried in vain to find a cure and a positive name for Maria's condition. They were so distraught that they temporarily forgot their Franciscan allegiance and resorted to fortune-tellers, strange medications, and magic. For her part, Maria reacted to her condition with anger and irritability. She resented her condition, with apparently no hope of a cure, and especially her inability to move, since the slightest change in position produced vomiting and vertigo.

Maria continued in this attitude until her aunt Annamaria journeyed to Grassano and paid her a visit. The aunt was highly respected in the area and was known as a deeply Christian woman. She spoke to Maria about the mystery of the Cross and instilled in her the value of suffering for herself, her neighbors, and the Church. Whatever else she confided to Maria, the little patient seemed to have changed and was granted the grace to accept her heartbreaking immobility.

Maria joined the Franciscans as a tertiary in 1953, and in 1954 she participated in the prayers of the Apostolate of Suffering and the prayers of the Feminine Division of Catholic Action. She suffered and sacrificed, frequently received Communion, and was faithful to her Franciscan vocation. She also joined the Apostolate of the Suffering and the Marian Crusade.

She was delighted and spiritually enriched when a Franciscan friar from the Monastery of St. Maria of Potenza became her spiritual director. He organized her day so that there were times for prayer and meditation. Times were also set aside for receiving visitors, who were beginning to come to Maria for advice, courage in their difficulties, and to ask for her prayers.

In the few moments she had to herself, she liked to listen to the radio, especially to programs that came from the Vatican. She was intensely interested in the life of the Church and the Second Vatican Council, which was then taking place. She also offered her sufferings for the unity of the Church.

Three times Maria was brought to Lourdes. But she relied completely on the will of God and wholeheartedly accepted her condition in a spirit of holy bravery when a miracle was not forthcoming.

When Pope Paul VI and the council spoke of dialoguing with other churches, Maria noted that the Anglican archbishop of Canterbury, Michael Ramsey, had paid a visit to the Pope. She wrote to the archbishop in England and received an answer. He offered her spiritual advice and suggested that she consider her bed an altar on which she was the sacrifice offered for the welfare of the Church. Maria accepted this advice and embraced it for the rest of her life.

Maria died quietly on Holy Thursday, April 7, 1966, at the age of twenty-seven. Because of the solemnity of the day, her funeral was a quiet one without bells, but with the participation of all the inhabitants of Grassano and crowds from nearby villages. Three clergymen participated in the funeral and at the graveside, where Maria was entombed on the property of the Vignola family.

The Diocese of Tricarico has concluded the diocesan process, with a view to the beatification of this victim soul, who spent fourteen years in suffering for the love of God, the salvation of souls, and for the good of the Church. †

Blessed Marianna Biernacka

1888–1943

Farmer, Mother of Two

POLAND

German forces marched into Poland on three fronts on September 1, 1939, acting under Adolf Hitler's order to kill "without pity or mercy, all men, women and children of Polish descent or language." During the next month, Polish Jews and non-Jews were stripped of all rights and subject to special legislation. Rationing allowed for only the smallest amount of food and medicine, Polish men were forcibly drafted into the German army, the Polish language was forbidden, and schools and colleges were closed. The Polish press was liquidated; bookshops and libraries were burned, as were churches and religious buildings; priests were arrested or sent to concentration camps. Street signs, cities, and towns were renamed in German, while community leaders were executed in public.

Of the eleven million Holocaust victims of World War II, an estimated six million were Polish citizens. Three million of these were Polish Catholics and other Christians.

Counted among this number was Marianna Biernacka, whose biography is very brief. She was born in the little Polish village of Czokalo, but documents concerning her birth are nonexistent. What little education she received was from family members, and it is known that she could never write. When she was about twenty years old, she married Ludwig Biernacka. Of her children only two survived, a daughter, Leokadia, and a son, Stanislaw.

Marianna and Ludwig were farmers who were assisted in their work when Stanislaw was old enough to help. In time, Leokadia married and moved away with her husband, but Stanislaw remained at home to help with the farm work. He, too, married, to a young farm girl named Anna.

The family was never politically active, neither before nor during the war. So they were quite surprised when German soldiers knocked at their door to arrest Stanislaw and Anna in retaliation for the death of German soldiers in a nearby village.

For Marianna, God and His law, and the dignity of life, were important values, even more valuable than her life and freedom. She stepped forward and begged to take the place of her daughter-in-law, who was pregnant. The soldiers accepted her urgent plea and allowed Anna to remain in the house, while Stanislaw and Marianna were taken away and imprisoned.

They remained in detention for only two weeks before their martyrdom on July 13, 1943, in Naumowicze near the town of Grodno. During her imprisonment, Marianna asked for only one thing—a rosary.

News of her heroic act greatly inspired people in nearby villages. Some who had already fled to the woods for safety remained in hiding, but those who stayed in their homes were determined to meet bravely whatever difficulties they would meet, in imitation of Marianna's sacrifice.

In time, a granite marker giving a few details of her martyrdom was placed at Marianna's farmhouse. Fifty years after her death, a memorial service was held for Marianna and her son, Stanislaw.

For the heroic act of offering her life for that of her daughter-in-law and her unborn grandson, Marianna Biernacka was beatified June 13, 1999, together with one hundred and seven Polish martyrs. †

Marica Stankovik

1900–1957

Founder of Lay Organization, Writer

CROATIA

$\mathcal{M}$arica Stankovik was born on the last day of the year 1900 and was accepted into the Church through the Sacrament of Baptism on the first day of the year 1901.

Living in a modest home in the Zagreb-Uppertown, Marica had a happy childhood, receiving from her family a solid Christian upbringing. Her education was entrusted to the Sisters of Mercy of St. Vincent, where her natural talents were developed and where she received a religious education that encouraged the progression of her spiritual life.

It was the sisters who first noted her gift for writing and her inclination to help others through Catholic organizations. She was very active in these organizations and eventually learned of a movement founded by Dr. Ivan Merz. She not only joined the movement, but remained good friends with Dr. Merz until his death. Throughout their friendship, he was her careful teacher. He helped her in her activities and inspired her spiritual progress, which left a deep impression on her life and her work.

Her goodness, sincerity, understanding of human nature, optimism, humor, and deep spirituality irresistibly appealed to youth. It was the foundation for her successes. So much confidence was placed in her that she became known throughout Croatia as "Sr. Marica."

By the time she was twenty-seven years old, she had become president of the Union of Croatian Female Youth, otherwise known as *Orlice*, or "Eagles." She was also active in an organization for women dedicated to the cross of Christ.

Because of her involvement in these organizations she traveled a great deal. She organized meetings and activities, visited other branches of the organizations, and lectured and wrote for Catholic newspapers about all the topics of her time, especially about subjects that would interest women. She also wrote about the Eucharist, the apostolate, the Church, and the pope, among many other topics.

Her motto was "For Christ, for the Church, for souls." Fully consecrated to God, Marica was so dedicated to helping others that, in 1938, with a small group of like-minded girls, she laid the foundation of a community that later developed into the first secular institute in Croatia. Named Associates of Christ the King (*Cooperatrices Christi Regis*), the institute received its official canonical approval in 1953 and is still very active today.

In 1942, her work received a high ecclesiastical recognition when she received the *Pro Ecclesia et Pontifice* award. The following year saw the publication of her book, *Mladost Vedrine* (*The Youth of Serenity*), which described her life and her organizational work.

During a sad time of political and religious upheavals in Croatia, Marica was arrested September 1, 1947, for fearlessly witnessing to her loyalty to Christ and His Church. Her public activities, as well as her sterling reputation as a Catholic, brought her to trial, and she was sentenced to five years in jail. She served the sentence in the correction institute in Slavonska and returned to Zagreb in 1952, with seriously damaged health. In spite of her many sufferings, she retained her diligence and her characteristically sweet smile.

During the next five years, she managed to educate a new generation of young associates of Christ the King. Marica died on October 8, 1957. Her last words were "Your grace will do."

Among the many inspirational documents she has left us are these encouraging words from one of them: "We should go forward calmly and confidently with a deep belief that the Lord's right hand leads everything, that all things have a meaning, although we can't see it now, but that we each have a role and mission in this life." †

The Martyred Women
of the Spanish Persecution
∽

1936–1939

When a Spanish republic was proclaimed on April 14, 1931, anticlericalism began immediately, with fires started in the churches of Madrid, Valencia, Málaga, and other cities. When the Popular Front began its activities in 1936, conditions became more grievous because socialists, communists, and other radical groups did everything they could to eliminate the Catholic Church altogether.

From the beginning of the persecution, Spain became the land of martyrs. The number of those killed for the faith is unknown, but we do know that the religious alone who were martyred represented thirty-seven dioceses. Pope St. John Paul II beatified two hundred thirty-three of these martyrs on March 11, 2001.

Of this number there were twenty-two women and twenty males who represented the then-flourishing Spanish Catholic Action. This group represented people of all ages and professions, who continued their apostolates in spite of threats, fear of arrest, and death. Here then are the twenty-two women beatified for sacrificing their lives for their faith.

Blessed Amalia Abad Casasempere (1897–1936) was a widow and the mother of two daughters. She was a domestic worker, dedicated to Catholic Action, and belonged to several other religious associations. She encouraged charitable activities in collaboration with her parish priest.

Blessed Ana Maria Aranda Riera (1888–1936) was unmarried and dedicated to the Church and the apostolates. She was deeply religious and attended Mass every day, and she was active in various associations and movements in the Church.

Blessed Carmen Garcia Moyon (1888–1937) was a tertiary of the Capuchin order and taught sewing and embroidery. She also taught catechism and faithfully cleaned the beautiful parish church. She participated in many social and parochial endeavors.

When **Blessed Consuelo Mella** (d. 1936) heard the news that her sister, Blessed Dolores Mella, was arrested, Consuelo went to the convent of the Escolapia nuns, where her sister had resided. Consuelo was soon arrested and died by firing squad. She was thirty-eight years old.

Blessed Crescencia Valls Espi (d. 1936) was martyred along with her three sisters. Her occupation was that of an embroiderer, and she participated in the life of the parish through various associations.

Blessed Dolores Mella (d. 1936) was martyred with her sister, Blessed Consuelo Mella. She lived with the Escolapia nuns, but never joined the order. She made a personal vow of celibacy and stayed with the nuns during dangerous times, doing their shopping under the threat of arrest. Dolores was thirty-nine years old at the time of her death.

Blessed Florence Caerols Martinez (1890–1936) was a textile worker and unmarried. A model of goodness to her fellow workers, she taught catechism in her parish and often visited the sick.

Blessed Francisca Cuallado Baixauli (1890–1936) was an unmarried seamstress. She helped many, even during the most difficult moments of the persecution, without ever hiding her Christianity.

Blessed Herminia Martinez Amigo (1887–1936) was shot along with her husband. She participated in numerous works of charity and was spiritually nourished on the Eucharist and the love of the Blessed Virgin.

Blessed Encarnación Gil Valls (1888–1936) was an unmarried teacher who impressed her students with an evangelical spirit due to her deep faith.

Blessed Josefina Moscardo Montalva (1880–1936) was unmarried and was generous to the needy. She continued her work, never hiding her condition as a Catholic medical instructor or her participation in numerous parochial associations.

Blessed Luisa Maria Frias Canizares (1896–1936) was an unmarried professor of the University of Valencia and well-known for her charitable spirit and social work. She developed an apostolate among the university students and helped in her parish.

Blessed Maria del Olvida Noguera Albelda (d. 1936) was unmarried and worked in various apostolic associations. She lived a deep Christian life and was very active in parochial and social issues.

Blessed Maria Climent Mateu (1887–1936) was martyred with her mother. She was a fervent Catholic who participated in parish activities and various associations.

Blessed Maria Teresa Ferragud Roig (1853–1936) was eighty years old at the time of her martyrdom. She had five daughters, four of whom were nuns. When the persecutors arrested the daughters, Maria bravely said, "Where my daughters go, I will go." She saw each of her daughters killed before she was likewise martyred.

Blessed Maria Jorda Botella (1905–1936) was an unmarried woman who radiated optimism and joy. She was active in the social apostolate and was charitable to the needy.

Blessed Maria Luisa Montesinos Orduna (1901–1937) was martyred with her father, her three brothers, and an uncle. She was a dedicated worker in the family and was active in many religious associations.

Blessed Maria of the Purification Vidal Shepherd (1892–1936) was unmarried and very conscious of her duties as a citizen and a Catholic. She was helpful to all and participated in an intense spiritual life centered on the Eucharist and the love of the Blessed Mother.

Blessed Maria del Carmen Viel Ferrando (1893–1936) was unmarried. She worked a great deal with the young and participated in the social activities of her parish, especially the religious initiatives.

Blessed Pilar Villalonga Villalba (d. 1936) was unmarried. She was deeply religious and was conscientious in the service of the Church through Catholic associations.

Blessed Sofia Ximenez Ximenez (1876–1936) was a widow with two children, martyred with two nuns, one of whom was her sister. She was the mother of an exemplary family and knew how to arrange her domestic duties to have time for apostolic commitments in her parish.

Blessed Tarsila Cordova Belda (1861–1936) was a widow who lost three children. She participated in the social apostolate, practicing charity with the sick and the poor. She advanced in the spiritual life by way of the Mass and daily Holy Communion. †

Servant of God Matilde Salem

❧

1904–1961

Philanthropist

Sʏʀɪᴀ

𝓜atilde Salem's wealthy family lived in Aleppo, Syria, but the family's fortune did not interfere with her prayer life or her steady progress in virtue. She married George Elias Salem in 1922 and was very happy, except that she found it impossible to have children. Also of great concern after almost twenty-two years of marriage was the fragile health of her husband, who died in 1944.

As a widow, she could have provided herself with an attractive life of leisure and transitory happiness. Instead, she sought out her true vocation, which was to devote herself to the welfare of others. The poor men of the city and the sick, she said, were truly her adopted children.

In collaboration with the Catholic Greek archbishop of Aleppo, Isidoro Fattal, they devised a grand plan to help in establishing commercial businesses in the capital that would aid the poor. She also donated her house to the children helped by the Salesians. It was named the Foundation George Salem, in honor of her deceased husband.

Matilde was active as a Salesian cooperator and joined the Third Order of St. Francis. In addition, she was cofounder of the association known as the Work of Infinite Love. She gave freely to charities, so much so that it was said there was not a charitable institution that she did not support. Some of these included the Society of Catechists, the Conference of St. Vincent, and the summer settlements for the poor and abandoned. She was also the vice president of the Red Cross and donated funds for the work among young delinquents.

On Pentecost Monday 1959, she was stricken with cancer. In reply to the physician's diagnosis, she made one comment: "Thanks, my God." She carried her painful cross for twenty months. She gave all her possessions to various works of charity, and since she had already given away her house, she was able to say, "I die in a house that is no longer my own."

Matilde died with a reputation of holiness when she was fifty-six years old. She and her husband, George, are entombed in the church of the Salesians in Aleppo, Sicily. Her cause was begun in 1994. †

Blessed Natalia Tulasiewicz

1906–1945

Teacher, Martyr

POLAND

$\mathcal{N}$atalia Tulasiewicz was a dedicated teacher in the Archdiocese of Poznan, Poland, and an enthusiastic worker in the apostolate of the laity.

Always deeply religious and concerned for the welfare of others, she wrote the following in her spiritual diary: "My mission is to teach people that the road to holiness is not to be found only in convents or pious families; it passes through noisy markets and traffic-laden roads of the world. . . . I want holiness for thousands of souls. It will not happen, it can never happen, that I will enter heaven by myself. After my death, I want to bring to heaven the vast number of people who die after me." Her dream was realized a few years later.

Natalia's last years were lived during a dreaded time in Poland's history (1939–1945), when the German occupation of her country was marked by arrests and deportations of Jews and Christians to concentration camps. It was during this time that Karol Wojtyla, the future Pope St. John Paul II, was forced to study underground for the priesthood. He and Natalia saw many of their friends and countless priests arrested for the sole reason they were Catholic.

It would take an extraordinary person with an extraordinary love of souls to forfeit one's freedom for that of a concentration camp, but that is exactly what she did. Her desire to help others was remarkable, since she voluntarily left with a group of women who had been sentenced to forced labor. Her aim was to work beside them to give them encouragement and religious assistance. When the Gestapo found out, she was formally arrested, tortured, humiliated in public, and finally condemned to death.

After her sentence, when she rejoined the women prisoners in their squalid barracks, she bravely climbed on a stool with the little strength that was left in her battered body and gave a talk on the Passion and Resurrection of Jesus.

Two days later, on March 31, the Nazis brought her to the gas chamber at Ravensbruck concentration camp, where she died in the company of many others.

Natalia is included in a group of one hundred and eight Polish martyrs who were beatified by Pope St. John Paul II on June 13, 1999, at Warsaw. The only other laywoman in this group was Blessed Marianna Biernacka, mentioned elsewhere in this book. †

Pauline Archer Vanier

1887–1991

Humanitarian

CANADA

$\mathcal{T}$he Canadian government recognized Pauline Archer Vanier in 1967 for her humanitarian deeds, an honor that countless people applauded as richly deserved. She was a woman of social standing with a well-rounded education, which prepared her to be a suitable companion in her diplomatic husband's activities. She worked tirelessly to relieve the suffering during World War II and for *L'Arche* (The Ark), her son's organization for the mentally and physically disabled.

Pauline was a lively, outgoing woman of extraordinary energy, both physically and religiously. She had a dazzling smile that pleased everyone and a noble bearing that indicated a strength of will and purpose. She was born to privilege and wealth in Montreal on March 28, 1887.

As a child she had always wanted to devote herself to a great cause. For a time she even entertained thoughts of a religious vocation, but this she promptly abandoned after meeting the dashing George Vanier, whom she married on September 29, 1921. At the time of the wedding, Pauline was thirty-one years old. George Vanier, who was born on April 23, 1888, was thirty-three.

They were blessed with five children: Thérèse, who became a doctor and worked a long time with elderly people at St. Christophe in London; George Benedict, who became a Trappist monk; Bernard, who was an artist painter; Michel, who worked as a translator; and Jean, who founded The Ark.

When Pauline married George Vanier, he was already an attorney who had served in the military and had been wounded in battle—a wound that resulted in the amputation of his right leg. He rose quickly in government, becoming at first an assistant to the Canadian High Commissioner in London, and then as a member of the Canadian delegation at the League of Nations in Geneva. He rapidly became a much-esteemed and respected diplomat.

He was named the Canadian minister to France, but while serving in Paris in 1939, he and the family had to flee when the German armies started their march through France. The family took refuge in England, where they turned their energies to helping the thousands of European refugees who also fled to England for safety.

Pauline immediately joined the Red Cross and began visiting hospitals. "I set out every day in an army car . . . to every hospital to find out where all the French wounded were. I found I could be particularly helpful to those who spoke no English, since only rarely did the hospital staff speak French."

The Vanier family was recalled to Canada, but in September 1944 they returned to Paris, with Pauline busily representing the Canadian Red Cross. The compassion of the couple was sparked by their deeply spiritual exercises. When they returned to Paris, they began to set aside a daily half-hour of prayer together, in addition to Mass and Communion.

Despite all their activities and a tiring public life, they developed a habit of meditation, said to have resembled that of monks and mystics. An observer once asked in astonishment, "Have you seen the Vaniers at prayer?"

A Canadian journalist wrote, "They are utterly rapt. Their whole hearts and minds are in a deep communication with God. Some say God is dead. How absurd. If God is dead, with whom are the Vaniers talking?"

While George gave many speeches on the radio to inform the Canadians of the situation in France, he urged the country to send clothing, shoes, and food for the displaced. For her part, Pauline organized distribution centers for the articles that arrived from Canada. During the year 2000, the Canadian postal service commemorated the Red Cross for its efforts at this time with a stamp that bore the likeness of Pauline Vanier.

Always concerned for the suffering and displaced, Pauline organized reception services at the train station for refugees and the homeless:

"We greeted them with drinks, refreshments, clothes, and survival kits, and tried to reach their families or anyone who might take them in. Many, however, had no idea whether anyone they knew was still alive, let alone their whereabouts. For them, we arranged temporary shelter. Then we took their photos and stuck these up on long panels, lining both sides of the railway station, in hopes that someone in the crowds would recognize the name or the picture of a long-lost relative or friend."

One of George's main concerns was to assist refugees, particularly the Jewish victims of the Nazis, in finding homes for them in Canada. Pauline's concern was to provide immediate help, sometimes in their own apartment. When Paris was liberated in 1944, Pauline, with the help of the Canadian government, provided a haven of comfort for wounded soldiers and orphaned children.

During this time, George was able to visit Buchenwald concentration camp. Afterward he broadcast an indignant and touching report to Canada. One report observed, "Tonight you put Christ on the airwaves."

By the year 1947, Pauline decreased her engagements at the Red Cross to devote more time to her obligations as the wife of an important and busy diplomat. Yet each Thursday, she retreated to the monastery of the Carmelite nuns for a few hours to renew her "spiritual batteries."

After George reached retirement age, the family left Paris in 1953 and established themselves in Montreal in a modest apartment, where they continued their social works of mercy. Their peaceful retirement did not last long. When George was seventy-one years old, the government once more called upon him, this time to serve as Canada's first French-Canadian governor general, a position he held for eight years, from 1959 until his death.

Before he assumed his duties, however, Pauline advised him to consult a doctor. George displayed his total trust in God by replying, "If I must fulfill this function, God will give me the force to achieve it. I do not need to consult a doctor."

On the day of his installation as the French-Canadian general governor of Canada, George wrote: "I request that we always work for the glory of God in simplicity and humility. It is not easy. But we entrust this to the merciful love of the Sacred Heart of Jesus. We count on your assistance to meet the tests that await us."

In this new position, George and Pauline traveled to all parts of the country, speaking on behalf of the poor, youths, and the family. Just as the French had been, the Canadians were somewhat in awe of this couple's Christian vitality, which was founded on daily participation in the Mass and reception of the Eucharist. They were also greatly influenced by the spirituality of St. Thérèse of the Child Jesus and endeavored to direct their lives according to the will of God and the example of this saint.

With all the activities and responsibilities of his office, George and Pauline found time in 1964 to organize what would become their main legacy: the Canadian Conference on the Family, which attracted more than three hundred scholars and experts. The following year saw the establishment of the Vanier Institute of the Family. Since that time, the institute has aided parents in need of counseling and helped others to deepen their understanding of what constitutes the quality of family life.

George once observed, "A close look at the family in Canada could help more people to find the warmth and delight we found ourselves."

During the 1960s, the Vaniers gave the country a vision of hope. Just three days before his death, George remarked, "One often hears the cries of distress of those who long for what they call the good-old times, but I tell you the good times are now. The best time is always the present time, because it alone offers the opportunity for action, because it is ours, because on God's scale it is apocalyptic."

When George died on March 5, 1967, the couple had been married forty-six years, years of mutual love, cooperation, closeness, and togetherness in their love of Church and their fellow man.

When the death of George Vanier was announced, the press and the media spoke about him as a great man who left an indelible mark on Canadian history. More than fifteen thousand messages of sympathy were received at the government house, many from children. One young boy, on returning from school, told his mother: "The flags are flying low today because a good man has died."

After her husband's death, Pauline returned to France to help her son, Jean, at The Ark, an organization he had established at Trosly-Breuil. This organization is a cooperative, self-help community that works with those who are mentally or physically disabled to help them live full and productive lives. Pauline loved her work among the residents and they loved her in return, so much so that they called her "Granny." Pauline worked there for twenty-four years, performing all kinds of menial work until her death in 1991 at the age of ninety-three.

Pauline's body was returned to Canada, where she was interred in a tomb next to that of her husband at the Citadel in Quebec. It is expected that their cause for beatification will soon be officially opened.

One journalist was to observe what countless others have thought, that the Vaniers had become "one of the noblest symbols of the Canadian journey." †

Venerable Pauline Marie Jaricot

1799–1862

Founder of Organizations

FRANCE

Although Pauline Marie Jaricot lived more than a century before most of the other women featured in this book, her memory conveys her to the present by those organizations she founded, which are still very much in operation. The Society for the Propagation of the Faith and the Universal Living Rosary both claim her as founder.

As the last of the seven children born to Antoine Jaricot and Jeanne Lattier, Pauline was born into wealth and privilege, her father being one of the leading silk merchants of Lyons, France.

Little is known of her early childhood except that, before she was seven years old, Pauline had received the blessing of Pope Pius VII as he passed through Lyons on his return from Napoleon's coronation as emperor of France. Her preparation for Holy Communion was described by one biographer as unfortunate, since Jansenism was then rampant in France. This was an extremely rigorous code of morals, consuming her young mind with the horrors of sin and doubts about forgiveness. We are told that for years she haunted confessionals, seeking assurance of God's mercy.

While growing into a young woman of great beauty, charm, and grace, she attracted the attention and admiration of many. Pauline was described by her contemporaries as being slightly above medium height, with a slender figure, dark eyes, and dark curls that framed her oval face. She was an excellent dancer and something of a flirt. She was the object of male attentions and female envy.

Pauline wrote, "I dressed myself in all my finery, believing myself worthy of universal admiration, and preening myself with the conceit of a peacock. Self-love made itself forcefully into my heart." As a result of wearing exquisite dresses and expensive adornments, she received all the admiration she expected. Pauline once wrote, "I would have had to be made of ice not to enjoy the flattery, compliments, and gentle words of praise I received."

She attended exquisite balls and enjoyed everything that elegant society provided. Of the many young men who sought her attention, only one succeeded in winning her heart, and for a time she was secretly engaged.

In the autumn of 1814, tragedy visited the beautiful Pauline when she reached for a box on top of her wardrobe and fell from a chair on which she was standing. Even though Pauline was in great pain, the doctors were unable to find broken bones. They knew of no remedy that would alleviate her suffering except for bleeding, which was then a popular medical procedure.

Unfortunately, this did nothing but cause anemia, weakness, and a general physical deterioration. Eventually she experienced convulsions, chest pains, body spasms, loss of weight, and erratic speech. She showly regained her health during an eight-month visit to the family's country estate at Tassin, which was located not far from Lyons.

Fully restored, she returned home to Lyons and resumed her participation in social events, but after enjoying these functions, she often began to cry for reasons she could not understand. She was now seventeen, and Divine Providence would soon change her life dramatically.

One day she dressed in one of her sumptuous outfits and, like many others who were also dressed exquisitely, she attended Mass in the Church of St. Nizier. There, Fr. Wendel Wurtz gave a scorching homily against vanity. Greatly affected, she visited with Fr. Wurtz who, for a time thereafter, served as her spiritual director.

Complying with Fr. Wurtz's advice, she began to visit the poor in their homes and in the hospitals. She sold her jewelry and other valuables and distributed the money to the needy. As a sign of her final break with the past, she gave her beautiful dresses away and clothed herself in a plain, purple dress that she disliked. Naturally shocked by this drastic change, the family cautioned Pauline to be more discreet and restrained.

Pauline wrote, "I took such extreme measures because, if I had not broken off all at once, I would not have done it at all. For the first several months, every time I met one of my girl friends dressed in the latest fashion I suffered bitterly. . . . I would never have been able to cure myself of vanity if I had not guarded myself carefully. Death seemed to me more preferable than renouncing all the vanities of the world."

Pauline attended daily Mass and advanced rapidly in virtue while serving the poor and working every day in the hospital of incurables. During Christmas week, in the year 1816, when she was eighteen, Pauline visited the Marian shrine at Fourviere, and while kneeling before the statue of the Blessed Mother, she pledged perpetual chastity.

While on a prolonged visit to her sister in St. Vallier, Pauline's ability to inspire others was exercised when she organized desolate and wayward girls of her own age and found work for them in the silk factory. To enable them to advance spiritually, Pauline organized them into an association known as the Penitents, or the *Reparatrices* (Women of Reparation). The members followed a simple rule of life and held regular meetings, during which they made plans to assist those poor or sick whom they knew were in need of help.

Pauline then turned her attention to a new system that would help foreign missions. In this endeavor she was encouraged by her brother, Philèas, who was studying to become a Sulpician priest. In the beginning, Pauline begged pennies from the two hundred *Reparatrices* at the factory. Within two years, she had completed her plan for a system of collections that Fr. Wurtz claimed must have been inspired by God.

The organization, established in 1822, consisted of collectors, each of whom was to ask for pennies every week from ten contributors. The collectors would then give the money to a director who would be in charge of many collectors. The director would finally forward the funds to a general committee. Known as the Society for the Propagation of the Faith, the organization finally became a worldwide agency, which now contributes millions to foreign missions.

Rather than remarking on the success of the organization, Church leaders now criticized it, since they felt that Pauline was meddling in Church business. Zealous Catholics, and even many priests, held her up to ridicule and accused her of monstrous hypocrisy. Other organizations, which endeavored to raise funds for a similar cause, proved to be envious of her accomplishments. Pauline finally quieted the vicious remarks by relinquishing her leadership of the organization to a board of directors, which was composed of leading Catholic laymen of Lyons.

Pauline next became seriously ill with a congested liver, an infected lung, and a bad heart. Although the prognosis was grim, she nevertheless recovered. Poor health was to return throughout her lifetime, as would harassment, criticism, and insults, from which she suffered miserably.

In 1843, Bishop Charles de Forbin-Janson of Nancy expressed his concern that millions of babies born in non-Christian lands were denied an opportunity to receive Baptism. So Pauline devised another plan: the Association of the Holy Childhood. Children, especially during schooltime, were asked to donate a penny a month and to pray daily for such babies.

This practice of caring for non-Christian babies is familiar to many who attended Catholic parochial schools. Over the years, millions of dollars collected by this association helped to build and maintain orphanages and schools in mission lands.

Since her "conversion," Pauline's interests had been to help the missions and to encourage prayer. With the Society for the Propagation of the Faith and the Association of the Holy Childhood both successes, Pauline's goal for the missions was realized. Her next interest was the propagation of prayer.

To accomplish this goal, she devised yet another association, a system of prayer known as the Association of the Living Rosary. Members of this organization were divided into groups of fifteen, with each member designated a particular mystery of the Rosary, whose decade was to be recited daily. In this way the group would collectively pray an entire Rosary every day.

The main objective was to pray for restoration of the faith for those who had lost it. A second objective was the distribution of good books and articles of piety. Twelve years after the founding, Pauline was able to inform Pope Gregory XVI that more than a million members were enrolled in the organization.

Once again, criticism was directed at Pauline by those who envied her success. Even though it was known that her wealthy father contributed generously to all her charitable endeavors, it was widely rumored that the money collected by Pauline was being used for her own selfish purposes. Pauline finally decided to quash the rumors by journeying to Rome to seek the approval of Pope Gregory XVI. While in the Eternal City she accepted the hospitality of the future St. Madeleine Sophie Barat, the founder of the Society of the Sacred Heart of Jesus.

Pauline became extremely ill during her stay in Rome and was diagnosed as having a growth on her lung. When Pope Gregory

XVI learned that Pauline was unable to go to him for an audience, she was granted the rare privilege of having the Pope visit her in the Convent of the Sacred Heart. After speaking about matters relating to the Propagation of the Faith and the Living Rosary, she overheard the Pope telling Mother Barat as he was leaving that he thought Pauline was dying. Pauline responded by telling the Pope that she intended to visit the shrine of the martyr Philomena to ask for a cure.

A few weeks later, still sick and weak, Pauline and her companions left Rome by carriage for the shrine of the early martyr Philomena in Mugnano, near Naples. While attending Benediction at the shrine, the thirty-five-year-old Pauline felt a surge of health. She stood up and was able to walk unaided from the church.

Two years earlier, Pauline had purchased a home at Furviere and named it Lorette, after the shrine of Our Lady of Loreto in Italy. The laywomen who lived there became known as the Daughters of Mary and labored with Pauline in assisting the poor. A frequent visitor to Lorette was the Fr. Jean Marie Vianney, the famous Curé of Ars, who not only shared an interest in the poor, but also had a great devotion to the Roman martyr, St. Philomena.

When he learned of Pauline's cure, he walked to Lyons to see for himself the wonders performed by St. Philomena. Pauline was privileged to have this future saint serve for a time as her spiritual director.

Once again, her organizational skills were used to help working men who were being denied an honest wage. Pauline devised a plan that would provide factory workers with better working conditions, eduction for their children, a Christian atmosphere in the workplace and at home, and a fair wage for their labors. Her dream was to establish a model factory town, whose organization and principles would inspire and result in many other ideal factory towns.

With the approval of the Curé of Ars, she enlisted the financial help of prosperous businessmen who invested in the plan. These funds were deposited in what she called the "Bank of Heaven."

When enough money was collected, Pauline bought a property called Rustrel.

To silence the critics who had formerly accused her of personally benefiting from money collected, Pauline hired two financial advisers, Monsieur Jean-Pierre Allioud and Monsieur Gustave Perre. Having known them previously, she had every reason to trust them implicitly, especially since Monsieur Perre came with a letter of endorsement from a priest at Apt. However, she eventually found that both men had embezzled money from the Bank of Heaven.

Perre, she learned, had paid off personal debts and had maintained a luxurious lifestyle. Pauline was then held accountable to the investors for the purchase price of Rustrel, as well as the interest on that amount since the day of purchase and the debts contracted by Perre. For the rest of her life, she labored to fulfill her promise to repay the full amount of the debts.

Pauline sold the Rustrel property in 1852 at a great financial loss. After the sale, she still owed a great deal of money and was forced to apply for a pauper's certificate. City authorities issued the certificate, which stated, "Pauline Marie Jaricot, living on the hill of Barthelemy, is in need and is receiving relief."

After she had exhausted every other means of raising money, her advisers insisted that Pauline ask for assistance from the Propagation of the Faith, based on her role as founder. The council adamantly refused to help, even when Pope Pius IX considered it only proper for them to do so and sent his cardinal vicar to the archbishop of Lyons to encourage the agency to help Pauline in her difficulties.

During her ordeal, the saintly Curé of Ars encouraged Pauline and gave her a wooden cross, on which was written, "God is my witness, Jesus Christ is my model, Mary is my support. I ask nothing but love and sacrifice."

Poor health returned to Pauline, who was now sixty-one years old. She continued her begging tours until her heart and lung condition made it impossible for her to continue. She also suffered from an increase in body fluids, which made her body grow larger and heavier. Her condition was so serious, her doctor held no hope for her recovery. Her companions at Lorette lovingly cared for her, and the poor whom she had helped in earlier times provided her with nourishing food.

The once wealthy and beautiful young girl, who had danced so gaily at parties, was now a woman reduced to abject poverty, poor health, and constant humiliation. She begged pardon of her companions for her faults on January 9, 1862, and cried out, "Mary, my Mother, I am all yours!"

These were her final words. Two days following her death, she was buried in the family crypt at Lyons, her cheap coffin accompanied by a crowd of the poor. After her death, the money obtained from the sale of Lorette satisfied all her debts.

The official decree opening the cause of Pauline's beatification was signed by Pope Pius XI on June 18, 1930. Five years later, Church authorities exhumed and examined the remains of Pauline Jaricot as part of the beatification process.

In official documents, Pauline Marie Jaricot is recognized as the founder of both the Society for the Propagation of the Faith and the Association of the Living Rosary. †

Blessed Pierina Morosini

1931–1957

Rape Victim

ITALY

$\mathcal{P}$ ierina Morosini was the only daughter and the firstborn in her family, which also included nine brothers. Her father, Rocco, was a guard and a farmer, and later in life an invalid. Her mother, Sara, a pious woman, also helped with the farm and supplemented their income by caring for other children. Born on January 7, 1931, Pierina lived a peaceful and prayerful life with her family on a small farm in Fiobbio, located in the Diocese of Bergamo in northern Italy.

She received the sacraments according to the custom of the time and was always a pious child. She was quick of mind and an excellent study. She also proved to be a willing assistant to her mother by helping with her brothers and performing chores, both inside the house and outside in the fields.

After finishing elementary school, Pierina enrolled in a sewing class and learned how to make clothes for the entire family. In addition to all the help she gave her family, Pierina wanted to assist them financially, and for that reason, when she was only fifteen years old, she began working at a cotton mill in nearby Albino.

A hilly, forested area separated the small town of Fiobbio and Albino, through which Pierina had to walk twice a day. She always recited her morning prayers on the path, received Holy Communion in the church in Albino, and then began her work at six in the morning. Her coworkers remembered her as cheerful with a sweet temperament, but not very talkative.

They also remembered her wearing clothes that were very plain and dark, and not in fashion. She once mentioned to them that she was not concerned with such. They also claimed that she seemed to work while in a profound union with God.

Always a very diligent worker, Pierina helped with the chores of the household after returning from a hard day's work. She was also an active member of Catholic Action, and at the age of sixteen she was named parish director of members in her age group. Pierina also distinguished herself among her townspeople by her devoted work on behalf of missionaries and the diocesan seminary.

She also assisted in the cleaning of the church and endeared herself to all because of her sweet disposition and humble demeanor. Her many works of charity are said to be the result of her deep prayer life, which was woven throughout the various parts of her day.

She always nurtured a profound attraction to the religious life and wanted to do missionary work among the lepers. Her aunt, who was a nun, recalled that when Pierina was a child, she told her, in all confidence, "I want to be a nun and belong to Jesus."

Because the needs of her family prevented her from leaving, she accepted the family's decision as the will of God and never spoke of her great disappointment. Realizing that Pierina might never be able to join the religious life, her spiritual director permitted her to make private vows of chastity, poverty, and obedience. To help herself maintain these vows as perfectly as possible, she wrote a twelve-point rule, which she observed for the rest of her life. In addition, she joined the Apostolate of Reparation, offering in a spirit of faith the many difficulties she encountered each day.

Pierina spent all her life in Fiobbio and Albino and never left except for a trip to Rome with members of Catholic Action for the beatification of Maria Goretti on April 27, 1947. During the journey, the life of Maria Goretti was the frequent topic of conversation, with all the travelers marveling how Maria had fought her attacker in the defense of her purity. When Pierina was asked what she would do if she were confronted by an assailant, Pierina quickly replied that she would willingly imitate Maria Goretti by dying in the defense of purity. On another occasion, she again stated that she would rather die than commit a sin.

After this trip to Rome, Pierina seems to have had a premonition that she would suffer martyrdom. Exactly ten years after the beatification of Maria Goretti, this premonition was realized. While she was on her way home from work on April 4, 1957, Pierina was confronted on the wooded path by a young man who seized her and dragged her off into the brush.

Judging from the condition in which she was found, and the many bloodied handprints in the area, Pierina had fought vigorously against the rapist and even attempted to crawl away. Found in the weeds nearby was a rock that was covered with blood and bits of flesh. It was in the shape of a hammer, and the assailant had apparently used this rock repeatedly to strike Pierina in the head.

Strange to report, on the day of Pierina's assault, one of her brothers had a premonition that something would happen to her and was very agitated concerning her welfare. For this reason he went along the wooded path to meet her after her work shift to accompany her safely home. Instead, he found his dying sister on the ground with her clothes in disarray and her long hair matted with blood.

As her brother drew nearer, Pierina slowly moved her hand to her head, but did not speak or open her eyes. Bending over her, he saw that her face was bloody and her breathing was slow and labored. When he touched the left side of her face, which was covered by her hair, his hand was immediately covered with blood and pieces of flesh. It was obvious that a huge and ugly wound covered the left side of her face and head.

The brother ran for help and returned with various relatives, who were shocked by what they discovered. It was then noted that the assailant had neatly arranged beside his victim her shoes, socks, purse, rosary, and a photograph taken of her with three of her friends.

Pierina was removed to a hospital, where she was treated for her injuries. But she lapsed into a deep coma and died two days later before she could describe or identify her assailant. Pierina was twenty-six years old.

Her doctors reported that she was a victim of sexual aggression, to which one of the doctors added, "We have here a new Maria Goretti." The Vatican newspaper *L'Osservatore Romano* (October 5, 1987), in its issue the day after her beatification, reported that, "Her skull was broken and she was raped." Pierina is, nevertheless, designated as "virgin," as well as "martyr."

Pierina's funeral was attended by most of the people of Fiobbio and Albino. The crime committed against her so outraged the people that it quickly became well known throughout the district. For this reason, an article on the front page of the newspaper of Bergamo told of her life and death and was accompanied by a picture of the huge crowd that attended the funeral.

A memorial marker and a stone to record the heroism of Pierina were soon erected at the place on the wooded path where Pierina had been found mortally wounded. A larger memorial stone, which is topped with a marble bust resembling Pierina, is found in the piazza of the church in Fiobbio.

The casket containing her remains were removed from her tomb on April 9, 1983, during the ecclesiastical examination into her life in preparation for her beatification. It was then carried in an impressive procession to the parish church of Fiobbio, where her relics are now entombed. This shrine attracts many of her devotees, who pray fervently for her intercession. It is customary for many of them to walk in procession to the place of martyrdom.

Pierina Morosini was beatified on October 4, 1987. Sara Morosini, Pierina's mother, had already met Pope St. John Paul II in 1981 but was privileged to meet him once again shortly after the beatification ceremony while he was still seated upon the papal throne. While Sara Morosini knelt before him, the Pope placed his hands upon her head and spoke words of comfort. After the ceremony, the Pope again spoke privately with her and then met with Pierina's brothers and other members of the family.

Kept as a treasured relic is Pierina's copy of a biography of St. Maria Goretti. It is said that this book was Pierina's favorite, and that she read it so often she almost knew it from memory.

Pierina has been recommended as a model for working girls and as a model of holy purity. †

Servant of God Praxedes Fernandez

1886–1936

Mother of Four, Abused Wife

SPAIN

*P*raxedes Fernandez, who lived a difficult married life, was in turn a wife, mother, a servant, and a widow. Her life began in the town of Mieres, in the heart of the Asturian mining valley in northwest Spain. Surrounded by huge mountains, the valley was, and still is, proud of its Catholic faith, its rich agricultural lands, and its natural resources of iron, mercury, magnesium, sulfur, and coal. The various mines of the region figure prominently in the life of this holy woman.

Her father, Don Celestino Fernandez, and most of his family worked in these mines, but he had other sources of income. He was a successful mining engineer and was the owner of land that he used for the production of lumber. He was a very good Christian, with his prominent virtue being charily. Not only did he contribute to the needs of the poor, but he also was called upon by his neighbors to arbitrate difficulties in the neighborhood, and even to restore peace in family arguments.

Praxedes' mother was Amalia Garcia Suarez, who was very good and generous to the poor. She was very thrifty in household matters and was a hard worker who was always busy. She was also very religious, as was her husband. Both participated in the frequent reception of the sacraments, and both conducted family prayers. In all, they seemed to be proper parents for a future saint.

Twelve children were born to this couple, but five died in infancy. Praxedes was the fourth to be born. A curious incident took place when Praxedes was twenty months old and still reluctant to walk.

Since her younger brother was then an infant, the mother, overwhelmed at having two babies to carry, turned to St. Rita of Cascia. While attending a Mass offered in the saint's honor, Amalia asked the saint for her intercession in the matter. On returning home, Amalia was relieved and very pleased to see Praxedes running to her with open arms. The sudden answer to prayer was considered a miracle by the neighbors. St. Rita was to be one of Praxedes' favorite saints throughout her lifetime.

Praxedes' life of charity began at the age of four or five, when a poor man knocked on the door of the Fernandez home and asked for something to eat. Praxedes ran to the kitchen, picked up a knife, and began to cut a loaf of bread, mutilating it in the process. The poor man was pleased, nonetheless.

Praxedes brother, Ismael, told later that "her religious inclinations were awakened in her at a very tender age." Her greatest joy during her childhood was the family Rosary. Her sister Celestina testified, "I know that Praxedes was the most fervent in praying the Rosary."

She was also an obedient child, never questioning commands, and was always alert to helping others. She also began at an early age to show an aptitude for good housekeeping, helping her mother around the house and caring for her younger brothers and sisters.

A month after receiving her first Holy Communion, Praxedes was faced with her first tragedy when her brother Hijinio, who was closest to her in age, died of diptheria at the age of six. It was then that she began to see the vanity of earthly things.

When she was eleven, the family moved to Sueros, her father's birthplace. Here they built a two-story house, with the upper floor used for the living area. The basement was converted into a delicatessen and a general store, with a bakery on the side that supplied the whole village. The delicatessen, the general store, and the bakery soon proved to be a very popular place for the village and surrounding areas.

There was also a sewing center, where many young ladies gathered to work. Praxedes willingly assumed the housekeeping chores and helped in the store. Besides this, she maintained two gardens, took sheep to pasture, helped in the bakery by kneeding the dough, and helped with the younger children. Hard work was to be the hallmark of her entire life.

With various chores incumbent upon members of the family, their home life was ideal. Neighbors noted the lively and jovial conversations, the music, singing, and dancing, and correctly named the house "The Neighborhood of Joy." Praxedes was a very happy person who loved to dance the *jota*, a Spanish folk dance, but she did so with moderation and modesty.

As Praxedes grew older, she never wasted time in useless playing and dancing, as did the other girls her age. She never missed Mass on Sundays and holy days. A remarkable child, Praxedes was always concerned for the poor, the sick, and the troubled, and she was always obedient and loving toward her parents and others. The delicacy with which she treated her parents was exemplary, especially during the times her father suffered from chronic stomach problems.

When Praxedes was about twelve years old, in January 1896, she attended school with the Dominican Sisters of the Annunciation, who were careful to give the girls a formation that corresponded to their future as wives and mothers. Her teachers have given us wonderful descriptions of Praxedes' life at this time. One teacher said:

"She was always very proper, and I know all the teachers held her in high regard. . . . She showed a great love for her mother and helped her at home with whatever had to be done. She was her father's favorite.

"Her sisters were good, too, but she had something special about her and was the best one of them all. Even at that young age she proved to be very pious. . . . She attended all the worship services, and she was always attentive to the sisters."

One of her classmates at this time later wrote of her: "I knew Praxedes at the Dominican Sisters' school . . . I noticed her virtuous conduct. I am convinced that even as a child she was so good. She fulfilled her duties, religious and otherwise, so well. She was often at Mass. I never saw her angry. Just by her ways one couldn't help noticing her humility."

Another former schoolmate wrote: "I got to know Praxedes from our school days. . . . No amount of praise could ever measure up to the reality of her goodness, for she was of a very religious character, very joyful, and extraordinarily humble."

Praxedes' sister Celestina once wrote of her: "She was the most fervent of all. In spite of the fact that there was much to do at home, she always accompanied our mother to the novenas of St. Rita and St. Anthony at six o'clock in the morning."

As an adolescent, Praxedes carried the heaviest load of the business. Her cousin, Benigna Fernandez, noted, "Not only in the house, she also worked out in the fields and with the animals. I used to see her from time to time carrying a basket on her head full of potatoes, onions, and other vegetables from the garden."

Praxedes was also the housekeeper, cook, baker, gardener, shepherd, and seamstress. "She never drew back from work." All this in addition to her favorite time-consuming religious exercises. A few years later she served her parish as catechist, with one of her students relating, "She taught with such dedication that we often prolonged the class past the time allotted. . . . She did this for many years."

When the Countess of Mieres and one of the nuns founded a program called Sewing for the Poor to provide clothes for the poor of the area, Praxedes joined and persuaded many young ladies to give their services gratuitously. When the Association of the Daughters of Mary was established in 1908 for unmarried young ladies, Praxedes enrolled the same day, and she was eventually named the first councilor of the association. She was also named choir director for the young women and was to remain an active member until the day of her marriage.

As a young lady, and even earlier, she attended daily Mass and received Holy Communion. She often made visits to the Blessed Sacrament. She also recited the daily Rosary and frequently made the Stations of the Cross. Later, in 1911, she joined the Archconfraternity of the Most Precious Blood, which led her to a great devotion to the Passion.

The daughters of the family eventually attracted the attention of young men, but Praxedes garnered the most attention. She was a very beautiful girl. She had red hair and clear blue eyes. She spoke little and was formal and refined. She wasn't interested in the latest fashions, but possessed all the qualities that a young man appreciates in a wife.

Although she had no interest in marriage and entertained thoughts of joining a convent, her spiritual adviser counseled otherwise. For this reason, she agreed to meet a number of young men. She refused them all until she met Gabriel Fernandez Martinez in her family's store.

Although he was not known for his economic or social standing, Praxedes saw goodness in him. He was an electrician by trade and a good man by all accounts. When he finally approached Praxedes' family with his proposal, the father dreaded the loss of his daughter, while the mother dreaded losing the help that Praxedes had always provided.

One day Gabriel said, "I wouldn't exchange Praxedes for any other woman in the world, be she queen or empress."

The wedding took place on April 25, 1914, when Praxedes was twenty-eight and Gabriel thirty-one. Praxedes was leaving her family who, because of hard work and thriftiness, had become wealthy. Now she was the wife of a simple man, whose earnings were meager.

After their honeymoon, they occupied a one-room apartment in the town of Figaredo, where Gabriel was close to his work. This apartment was in the home of a woman with three children. The kitchen was shared, but there was never a disagreement between the women.

Praxedes soon found that Gabriel was satisfied with the minimum of religious observances and was far from the ideals of his wife.

Was Praxedes an abused wife? We know that Gabriel developed a violent temper, and that Praxedes never told her mother-in-law of the treatment she received. One incident surfaced, however.

It took place on Good Friday in 1915, after Praxedes returned from church services, which Gabriel thought occupied too much of her time. In a fit of rage, he slapped Praxedes. The owner of the house witnessed the assault and promptly told Gabriel's mother, Filomena. Indignant over this, Filomena immediately went to see if it were true.

Praxedes' only words were these: "Gabriel is very good to me, and I have nothing to say against him." Filomena appreciated Praxedes' goodness and replied, "How good and holy Praxedes is. My son is not worthy of her."

Filomena confronted Gabriel about the matter, and a slight change of disposition took place. Praxedes was able to calm the flare-ups of her husband, and little by little his manner softened. Gabriel later commented, "I am happy to have taken her as my wife. I am entirely satisfied and live very contented with her."

Ten months after their marriage, Gabriel and Praxedes welcomed their first child, whom they named Celestino, after Praxedes' deceased father. After the child's baptism, Praxedes offered him to the Mother of God. Soon after, the couple moved from the one-room apartment into a two-story home with a yard and a garden.

Happily, Praxedes grew her own vegetables and flowers and spent many hours sewing for the family. The following year, 1916, saw the birth of Arturo. Enrique was born in 1917, and Gabriel in 1920. All of them were consecrated to the Blessed Virgin Mary.

Praxedes' married life presented many opportunities for the practice of virtue, as evidenced by what took place when Gabriel began to frequent a nearby tavern. It was then that his love for his wife cooled. Praxedes' cousin, Consuelo, testified:

"I saw Gabriel treat her quite harshly at times, despotically and disdainfully, as though he did not appreciate her. At times like this, Praxedes, who was always sewing, without ever answering him or defending herself, would just lower her head and cry."

A neighbor declared that "Gabriel made it hard on Praxedes, but . . . she never complained or said anything to anyone. Only once did she confide her problem to a paternal uncle, who recommended that she notify Gabriel's mother."

Filomena apparently spoke to her son about his behavior, since there was a complete change, and never again did he visit the tavern. Gabriel was certainly not a perfect husband. His meager salary, always a problem, nevertheless did not prevent him from frequently taking his friends to lunch. He smoked a great deal and was not inclined to save money.

Through all these difficulties Praxedes continued her prayer life, went to daily Mass, prayed the Rosary, and made frequent visits to the Blessed Sacrament. In addition, she seemed always to pray while occupied with her household duties.

One day, Praxedes had a premonition that her husband would soon be taken from her. That took place when two freight cars loaded with bricks became detached, rolled downward, and hit the locomotive where Gabriel and a stoker were crushed to death.

Without her husband's income, Praxedes turned to her family. Amalia, her mother, was now a very wealthy woman. All the members of the family were prosperous except Praxedes. It was understood that her father had provided for his daughters if any became widowed. Amalia, however, refused to part with the money, and to settle the matter, advised Praxedes to move into her home with her children, one a mere infant.

This move did not please Praxedes' younger sister, Florentina, who still lived at home. One day, Florentina commented, "It would be better if you and your children would go and leave mother and me in peace."

To this Praxedes softly replied, "If I receive the inheritance that is coming to me according to father's dying wish, I will be happy to leave. Otherwise, I have nothing to live on."

Florentina made it known that she resented Praxedes in the house and that she had no rights. She constantly ridiculed Praxedes and frequently found fault with her. At one point, she even locked a cabinet that contained some of her favorite foods. Praxedes saw to it that her sons ate all she could provide for them, but she often ate leftovers and often ate a meal of only bread and milk.

With Praxedes' return home, the maid was dismissed, and she assumed all the care of the house. In all respects she became a servant. With no income, she was forced to wear the cast-off shoes of her mother and sister, and she made all the boys' clothing from the clothing left by their father.

One of Praxedes' sons later reported, "My mother did all the heavy housework and even worked in the garden. My mother was the one who always served at the table and ate after all had eaten. She was the last to retire, and never before midnight. In other words, she was the servant of the house."

With the death of her mother-in-law, Praxedes received her home as an inheritamce, which she rented, providing her a little income of her own. Around this time, Praxedes began to assist at three Masses a day, two in Mieres and the third in Fabrica, having walked the distance between the two churches. In the 1930s, she said: "After receiving Holy Communion, I feel a tremendous heat in my breast." It would seem that Praxedes was receiving extraordinary graces.

Around the year 1927, anti-religious feelings were invading the valley, with diabolical sentiments expressed against all who were consecrated to God. Praxedes did what she could for the Church by helping the parish priest. Her charity toward the sick and poor increased as her own children brought home children who had been begging on the street. Praxedes delighted in feeding and clothing these poor unfortunates.

The following year, in spite of communistic anti-clericalism, Praxedes' son Enrique entered the Dominican seminary, much to Praxedes' pleasure, since she had always wanted one of her sons to become a priest. Once when she visited Enrique in the seminary, one of the priests, Fr. Felix Velez, to whom Praxedes went to confession, told one of the mothers, "Enrique's mother is a saint." Praxedes joined the Third Order of St. Dominic, an organization for the laity, during the last years of her life.

Arturo, the little rascal of the family, had earlier abandoned school to work in the mines. He was killed by a train, dying in almost the same manner as his father. Through this tragedy, Praxedes found a measure of solace in her faith and trust in God's mercy.

When money was given her for flowers, she invested it instead in thirty Gregorian Masses for the repose of his soul. During the third Gregorian Mass offered for Arturo, Praxedes saw her son in the arms of the Blessed Virgin, wrapped in her scapular. Full of joy, Praxedes returned home, and said, "Now I am happy, for my son has been saved."

During this time, when doors were closed to priests because of the communist hatred for anything religious, people refused to let their dying receive the last sacraments. Praxedes filled this void by assisting not only the sick, but also the dying, whom she prepared for death as best she could. Praxedes was permitted to perform these acts of charity because of her reputation for holiness, her sweet disposition, and her genuine love of others.

In imitation of St. Teresa of Ávila, whose writing had become familiar to her, Praxedes fasted, following the constitutions of the Discalced Carmelites and the great saints of the Church. On Fridays, she ate only one tablespoon of chickpeas, and on Saturdays she fasted on bread and water. Candy, which she loved, she permitted herself on one day only—Easter Sunday. All of these penances exasperated her family, who vocally objected on a number of occasions.

Financial relief came to Praxedes when her brother gave her a substantial amount of money. In addition, she received money for Arturo's death, and this, together with the small rent she received from the house she inherited, permitted her to help the poor generously. She assisted them by leaving money under the pillows of the sick whom she helped.

Praxedes once commented, "Charity is not practiced with leftovers for the poor. The best quality and quantity should be served to them just as to any relative."

Testimonies abound of Praxedes' aid to the poor and even the contagious sick, and to those in need of the sacraments. All who knew Praxedes were extremely grateful for her help and regarded her as a saint. One beggar called her "the mother of the poor." This declaration must have amused Praxedes.

When typhoid and intestinal infections drifted as a plague through the neighborhood, Praxedes became one of the victims. Dysentery and vomiting took hold of her, and she was forced to remain in bed. This was the first time she had been seriously sick.

In addition to these problems, appendicitis also caused pain, which she offered for the love of God. Finally, peritonitis set in with its terrible pains, which she suffered without even a groan. After several days, Praxedes died quietly, with two priests in attendance. Amalia, Praxedes' mother, exclaimed in her grief, "This daughter of mine was a saint."

The burial took place the next day, October 7, the Feast of the Holy Rosary. Because of the civil war then harassing Spain, multiple burials took place at one time. Afterward, all who had been buried in the Old Cemetery at Oviedo were transferred to a common grave in the modern cemetery of San Esteban de la Cruces. For this reason, the grave of this holy woman has never been located, but it was later determined that she had been buried where the diocesan seminary of Oviedo proudly stands today. †

Servant of God Rachel (Lina) Noceti

1898–1918

Tailor

ITALY

*R*achel Noceti was born into a family of modest social position in Genoa. When her father was stricken with a long and serious illness, she had to interrupt her schooling to help in the support of the family. She must have shown an aptitude for sewing, since she was sent, at the age of twelve, to learn tailoring. She studied and worked under eight different masters in various shops.

She worked diligently and neatly, according to her teachers and members of her family. At times, she was obliged to continue her work into the night and sometimes in the bitter cold, but she worked with a picture of the Sacred Heart of Jesus before her.

Together with the teachers and fellow workers of the shop, she recited the Rosary, and this was for her a pure joy. Unfortunately, since she was of a frail constitution, the strain of the work, the long hours, and the cold affected her lungs. She became so sick when she was nineteen that the Sacrament of Anointing of the Sick was administered to her.

She was taken to the hospital, first to Pammatone and then to San Martino, where the hospital chaplain permitted her to take the vows of poverty, obedience, and chastity.

She received the sacrament for a second time and died on April 3, 1918, at the age of twenty. She was first buried in the cemetery of Staglieno, but a solemn translation took place, with her final resting place in the church of St. Maria Maddalena, the parish church where she had been baptized.

The last action taken on the cause for Rachel's beatification took place in 1992. †

Servant of God Rosa Giovannetti

1896–1929

Musician, Concert Artist

ROME

*R*osa Giovannetti's father, the lawyer of Pope Leo XIII, provided a deeply Christian atmosphere for his family. In those
loving surroundings, Rosa demonstrated a particular aptitude for
devotion and music and was already, at the age of eight, studying
the piano and cello in the school of the celebrated professor Forino.
Under his instructions, she became a brilliant performer and received
a diploma in cello from the Academy of St. Cecilia. After numerous
concerts in Rome she became, at the age of twenty-four, a cellist in
the Costanzi Theater (today the Theater of Opera), displaying
in that environment a testimony of purity, goodness, and faith.

But music was not her only interest. She also loved sports, particularly boat racing and swimming, having competed at times in
swimming races. She was vivacious, with a charming personality
that made her dear to all.

Around the age of twenty-four, there appeared another facet of her personality. She seemed to like seclusion, but then there developed a great devotion for the apostolate. She soon yearned to consecrate herself wholly to God, and with the permission of her confessor, she pronounced a vow of chastity. Later, she secretly took vows of poverty and obedience.

She offered everything for priests and sinners and multiplied her works of charity to assist the fugitives from the war and those from a recent earthquake. She gave innumerable benefit concerts to help the nurses who assisted the poor and the sick. Her activities increased: She worked for the Apostolate of Prayer; was a Franciscan tertiary of Ara Coeli; worked as a catechist; founded a social organization named the Circle of the Female Youth of Catholic Action; and was engaged in other apostolate efforts.

Following a pilgrimage in 1927, she developed symptoms of a rare, incurable ailment that covered her whole body with bloody sores and produced almost unbearable pain. Confined in the St. Gallicano Hospital, she always seemed serene and even pleased, much to the surprise of her visitors.

Rosa died on January 30, 1929, at the age of thirty-three. Her remains were transferred in 1968 to St. Carlo of Catinari, where they are found in an ornate sarcophagus in the chapel of the Academy of St. Cecilia.

The informative process for her cause of beatification was approved in 1974. †

Rose Prince

1915–1949

Native American of the Dakelh People

CANADA

$\mathcal{I}$n 1951, four men opened graves and moved several remains from a small cemetery that was considered to be too close to the barn of the Lejac Residential School. The cemetery was near Fraser Lake, in the area known as British Columbia, in southwestern Canada. They were prepared to find yet another skeleton when the lid of Rose Prince's coffin, buried two years earlier, collapsed.

Revealed was the perfectly preserved body of a Native American woman. All the other graves revealed remains that had conformed to the laws of nature, with one grave being only a year old. One of the grave diggers said that the excellent condition of the body was a shock and made him somewhat scared. "But I soon realized that this must be a very special person." As to the condition of the skin, he related that it was soft and clear and looked somewhat warm.

The parish priest was promptly notified, as were the Sisters of the Child Jesus at the school. Eventually, the casket was brought to the school for the sisters and the students to examine. Sr. Eleanor Klusa, who saw the body, remembered Rose as a former student and recalled: "There was not a spot on her face, not a mark on her. She was such a lovely person. The flowers she was holding had wilted, but she was just lying there, all propped up on her pillow, with a little smile on her face."

Although the preservation of a body is remarkable, it is never considered of such importance as to recommend canonization on its own merits and is actually incidental to the consideration of the person's life and holiness. Yet at times, the good Lord seems to use the finding of a preserved body to draw attention to a life of great virtue that might otherwise have been overlooked.

It is said by Fr. Jules Goulet, who has investigated Rose's cause, that many visited her grave before the discovery of her preservation. But it might be that God meant for a greater devotion to be encouraged to this worthy young woman by the preservation of her body.

Rose belonged to a Native American tribe known as the Carrier Nation. She was the third of nine children born to Jean-Marie and Agathe Prince in Fort St. James. Her father was the descendent of a long line of Carrier chiefs and was so faithful in performing duties for the parish church that he was additionally known as the "church-chief."

At seven years of age, Rose began attending the Lejac Residential School. When she was nine, tragedy struck. One report has it that she fell from a swing and injured her back. But according to a childhood friend who witnessed the accident, Rose was leaning over to change her shoes when someone carrying a large bench lost control of it.

He was unable to prevent it from falling, and one end of the bench fell heavily against Rose's back. All suspected that her back had been broken. It is not known whether she was examined by physicians, but the injury caused her almost constant pain and produced a terrible deformity.

At the tender age of nine, she was known as a peacemaker between feuding children and was admired for her compassion. Her cousin Evalie Murdock recounted that often she "felt resentment toward other girls or one of the sisters, but then Rose would talk to me and say to pray for the person instead of feeling resentment. . . . She was full of good advice, good spiritual advice."

Her childhood best friend remarked that Rose was "very humble, but also had a nice sense of humor." Another friend told that Rose "was very ill from that accident," but added emphatically, "She never complained." Still another friend remembered that Rose was "quiet, nice, and sensitive to the feelings of others. . . . She was special to the Sisters and her schoolmates, who looked up to her and respected her."

A cousin recalled that Rose was gentle and patient, and that all brought their problems to her, since she gave such good advice. "She was a wonderful person. . . . I pray to her to pray for me."

Another cousin remembered that Rose was kind and gentle, and that people were always asking for her advice. "She didn't complain." When asked if she thought Rose was a saint, she remarked firmly, "She was a saint! She had the patience of a saint!"

Added to this is the opinion of Sr. Bridie Dollard, who taught Rose for three years. She recalled that Rose had to endure many trials and sorrows during her life, and that she developed a curvature of the spine that was painful. "Rose was very self-conscious about it," she said. The abnormality caused her great difficulty, yet all who gave testimony about Rose agreed that never once was she heard to complain. Sr. Bridie described her as "a hard worker and a brilliant student, kind, lovely, gentle, and compassionate."

When Rose was seventeen years old, her mother contracted influenza and died. In time, her father remarried, but when Rose returned home during vacations from school, she learned that her stepmother did not care for her, and probably never would. From then on, Rose stayed at the school and eventually graduated.

When she expressed the hope that the sisters would permit her to stay at the school and work, she was delighted that she would be a member of the staff. When asked why she never went home, she remarked that she had the sisters, and "I've got family here: our Blessed Mother and her Son, Jesus. They are my parents. I feel so close to them that I don't want to go away."

Rose's duties at the school were cleaning, secretarial work, mending, sewing, and helping with young children, who loved and deeply respected her. She also painted and embroidered flowers on altar cloths, vestments, and greetings cards. Others tell that they never heard a cross word from her, and that she did her tasks with great cheerfulness. "Rose loved to sing, and always sang or hummed while she was doing her chores. Her fingers were always busy with bead work or crocheting."

Since she was not one of the nuns, she was exempt from their religious practices. Nevertheless, she faithfully received Jesus at daily Mass and was noted for the many hours she spent kneeling in adoration despite her pain.

Finally, when Rose was in her early thirties, she became ill with tuberculosis, and by 1949 she was bedridden. In August, she told Sr. Francis that she was going off on a holiday, and that the sisters would never see her again. She was taken to the hospital at Vanderhoof, where she was admired for her patience and serenity. Rose died peacefully on August 19, after receiving the Holy Eucharist during a Mass that was being offered for her in the downstairs chapel.

The sisters prepared her body for burial, and because her body lay in an awkward position due to her deformity, they put a large pillow under her head and placed her body, with some difficulty, in the proper position. Rose was buried the next day, on her thirty-fourth birthday, in the Lejac cemetery during a simple ceremony.

Because the condition of her preserved body was discovered during the first week of July (two years after burial), the anniversary is observed every year with a three-day pilgrimage, which is attended by a large number of devotees, in addition to members of the clergy and the bishop. During this observance, the simple little fence that surrounds the grave is topped at night with countless burning candles, representing the love and prayers of her family, friends, and those seeking her intercession.

Fr. Jules Goulet noted, "The people around Fraser Lake have received many, many favors through her intercession." One astonishing miracle of healing has been repeatedly mentioned in the press. This miracle, as well as some others, have been effected by the application of dirt from Rose's grave.

It has been noted that, since the beginning of the pilgrimages in the 1950s, never once has the event been delayed, hampered, or touched by rain. †

Servant of God Santa Scorese

1968–1991

Martyr of Purity

ITALY

Santa Scorese's elementary schoolteacher once wrote this about Santa's disposition: "Extroverted and courageous, responsible, intelligent, willing, she establishes serene and affectionate relationships." Her mother recalled that she was indeed an extrovert, always "shouting a little when she arrived, 'Hey, good morning! Hi!' Everything was a bit like this. You felt her presence. She brought great joy wherever she went. It was her character, her way of living."

Another said that she was "full of enthusiasm." A former classmate agreed: "She was sincere and determined, good but a stubborn girl, who dared to talk about God among unbelievers and blasphemers, with incredible tenacity and sincerity." With so much spirit and such endearing ways, she had many friends who found it a joy to be near her.

Her mother, Angela Scorese, reported, "Sometimes she made me reprimand her. She put me in a situation to scold her, but then, after ten minutes, everything had passed; she would hug me and kiss me, coming up from behind."

Her father, Piero Scorese, was a police constable who reported that Santa, "from childhood, was a normal child like all the others, a bit lively. Then she went to school, she went regularly, she was fairly good. . . . She always found ways to convince me of anything."

She was born February 6, 1968, in Bari, and had a sister, Rosamaria. The father told that the two girls "spent their lives as children in the parish. It seemed normal to us that Santa went to Mass every day. We were really happy; we felt very fortunate."

During her fifth year of high school, she attended a course given by the Red Cross and took care of children suffering from polio and muscular dystrophy. During this time, she became acquainted with the Missionaries of the Immaculate, which opened new horizons for her. She often asked herself, "What does Jesus want from me?"

When she was seventeen, she attended a meeting in Rome of the Focolare movement, where Chiara Lubich, the foundress, addressed the group. Santa decided that this was what Jesus wanted of her. Her friend Roberta Carbone said, "What touched us immensely was this relationship with Jesus in the Eucharist that we were already living, but with a new light. It was really such a great joy that we hugged each other." Another friend in the movement said that Santa, almost immediately after joining the movement, participated in a musical group that was formed at Bari with some of the girls.

Rosamaria, Santa's sister, noticed that there was a new development "as she surrounded herself with people that she knew in the movement. . . . Her praying was more intense . . . she was more secure, stronger, more generous."

With some of her friends, she began to visit the town's old-age home, realizing that the elderly were symbols of Jesus' forsaken.

Her visits were so appreciated that one old gentleman, Mr. Aldo, pronounced her name before he died.

Santa moved with her family to Palo del Colle, a large agricultural center a few miles from Bari. There she started the study of medicine, since her ambition was to make herself useful to the poor, the sick, and the suffering. After a year, however, and following thoughtful consideration, she enrolled instead in the Department of Education.

For some time now she had kept a diary, in which she revealed her struggles and her love of God. It is through her writings that we discover the purity and beauty of her soul. She once wrote: "I would like to live like a lily, to enjoy the abundance that You give. I would like to be a sail that plows the seas, the oceans, that loses itself completely in Your immensity. I would like to have the wings of an eagle and fly up always higher toward You. I would like to be music that reaches Your ears and brings You joy."

One day, Santa consulted Irene Camimeo of the Focalare movement about a confusion she had regarding her vocation in life. She felt called to be one of the Missionary Sisters of Father Kolbe, but at the same time she wanted to continue with the movement. Irene recalled, "I had to wonder, to see how a girl so young had this strong sense of doing only what God wants. It was also a gift for me."

Fr. Tino Lucariello at this time related: "I think this experience with the Focolare movement, this spirituality, profoundly marked her spiritual journey. At this point, I would also say, her vocation."

With peace of soul restored, she was, however, deeply troubled about a serious problem that developed. A deranged young man began following her everywhere, pestering her in many ways and even threatening her. In time, his attentions became a real persecution. Santa was no longer free to move about unless she had a companion. The young man began to phone her and to write her letters, which she did not want even to touch.

Once when speaking to her friend Roberta Carbone, she said, "It's a suffering for me to live because it seems as if the Devil really has it in for me. He is making me undergo the hardest trials. This person wants me to abandon my ideals, to leave the Church, to leave everything . . . and only after that will he leave me in peace. But I'm not willing to do this. I would rather die."

Fr. Tino again related that Santa "was conscious of confronting death—of this I am certain. . . . We certainly have to highlight these spiritual qualities of Santa, especially her profound readiness, her evangelical radicality and her awareness of truly dying for Christ. After a private talk, one of our last talks, she had completely put herself in the hands of God."

On the evening of March 15, she had convinced her friends that she felt safe in driving home by herself. In spite of all her precautions, and even reports to the police, the young man hid in the shadows by the gate to her home and grabbed Santa as she passed by. When Santa struggled against his advances, he displayed a knife and inflicted twelve stab wounds. At the hospital, the doctors discovered that the knife had cut the pulmonary vein, resulting in a critical situation. Although they hurriedly attended to her, Santa died in the operating room.

After the funeral, Fr. Tino related that Santa's death "without doubt has brought much fruit in many people." Already, there have been favors granted through the intercession of this young martyr of purity.

Santa Scorese's sause for beatification has been accepted, with the last action being made on March 31, 1998. ✝

Servant of God Santina Campana

1929–1950

Victim Soul

ITALY

*T*he desire to love Jesus and Mary came early to Santina Campana, who was born into a peasant family at Alfedena (the Aquila). Even her spirit of self-denial made itself known when she was eight years old and working in the hayfields with her father and older sister, Maria.

To the shock of her father and sister, Santina's hands began to bleed from striking sharp stones. While Maria complained about her own hands and their fate, which forced them to work so hard, Santina replied that Maria should not worry, that God created the stones and knew that they would someday touch them and gain merits. "Besides," she replied, "it is not so much the stones since the skin of my hands and arms is very thin."

When she was old enough, she began to instruct the children of the parish in preparation for their first Holy Communion and

Confirmation. She also gave lessons on how to attend holy Mass properly and how to recite the Rosary correctly.

Santina became ill with pleurisy at the age of thirteen and endured its effects for eleven months. Realizing that the clean air of the mountains of the Abruzzi would help her condition, she moved there. But she continued to suffer atrocious pains, which were accompanied by high fevers.

The family remained in the region because of World War II and were forced to live in a stable, which placed other burdens on the little patient. In addition to the pleurisy, she endured hunger, cold, suffocating air, and conditions tolerable only to a person of faith.

She was always supported in her sufferings by her mother and sisters and, in spite of her condition, she maintained a peace and serenity that could be attributed only to the grace of God. After all, she reasoned, didn't Jesus live for a time in a stable?

Eventually, her condition became so critical that all suspected she would die. In response to their apprehensions, Santina declared that she was not afraid, and that all would take place in God's good time, if that was His will for her. While living in the stable, French troops came upon the place and gave Santina medicines that seemed to relieve her condition.

With the return to her native village at the end of the war, Santina seemed delivered of her ordeal, so much so that at the age of fifteen she expressed the desire to enter the religious life. That same year she joined the Sisters of Charity in Rome. After months of intense study and with angelic fervor, she began her novitiate. Two years later, however, on March 25, 1947, she vomited blood, which revealed the return of her pulmonary distress and the end of her life in the convent.

A few months later, Santina entered the sanatorium, *Rinaldi Villa* of Pescina, but she was not a sad or a disconsolate patient. Instead, she was vivacious, encouraging the other patients to prayer and love of God. Even when she began to lose weight alarmingly, and was repeatedly spitting up blood, she supported the others with her courage and her willing acceptance of pain as coming from the hands of God.

From her bed of pain, which she called "her white throne," she found initiatives to help the foreign missions and was able to send small contributions to them. She joined the Catholic Union of the Sick and sent messages of faith and love to all the members.

Unafraid of death, she looked forward to "flying into the arms of my Creator." She died on the evening of October 4, 1950, at the age of twenty-one.

One of those present later wrote, "How beautiful was Santina in her sufferings." Another wrote: "We contemplated Santina in her eternal sleep. How beautiful she was."

The chaplain of the sanatorium, Fr. Giacomo Michelin, who assisted Santina, added that he was fascinated by her candor and "the force of her mind, which was irresistible in her last days. The companions who gathered around her bed reported that she had a singular force of spiritual attraction. . . . Santina had lived as a saint and died as a saint, and now she can be found among the virgins of paradise."

Since her death, celestial favors reported through Santina's intercession have increased in number. The ecclesiastical authorities opened her cause for beatification in June 1979. †

Servant of God Satoko Kitahara

∽

1929–1958

Junk Dealer

JAPAN

The secular saints in this volume practiced virtue in such varied professions as medicine, law, teaching, organizing lay societies, lecturing, among many others. Satoko Kitahara's cause for beatification is being considered because she attained holiness in, of all places, a junkyard.

Known as Mary of Ant Town, Satoko was never really poor. She was born in Suginami, an affluent Tokyo suburb, in 1929, and her father, Kinji, was a descendant of generations of Shinto chief priests. He had earned a doctoral degree in agriculture and taught in that field. Her mother, Eiko, came from a wealthy family.

Since the Japanese revere their teachers as members of a sacred profession, Professor Kinji Kitahara enjoyed great respect. Additionally, he earned a generous income from a family shoe business. Satoko's home was comfortable, and it contained a garden so beautiful it was referred to by their neighbors as "The Flower Manor." Satoko, as well as her two sisters and brother, were well educated.

The girls especially were taught all that Japanese society expected of young ladies of breeding. The three girls learned that, in the Japanese family, the brother came first. As proper Japanese young women, they presumed their parents would arrange their marriages, and once wedded, they would walk behind their husbands. As good wives, they would never offer an opinion. When she became a mother-in-law, she would run her household with a firm hand.

Satoko, however, was a highly intelligent girl. She would not follow the path of life expected of her, which must have surprised and shocked members of her family.

During World War II, the teenage Satoko joined the war workers at Tokyo's Nakajima aircraft factory. With American bombers pounding Tokyo, she almost died more than once at her factory bench. Her father entered the armed forces, and her brother enlisted for factory work.

Government authorities urged their people to work unceasingly for the war effort despite the bombings. Workers often succumbed to overwork, including Satoko, who once collapsed from exhaustion and tuberculosis. Her brother, however, died of exhaustion.

After the war, with the influx of American soldiers and American women who served in all ranks of the military, the attitudes of the young Japanese changed. They became infatuated with the Americans' more relaxed way of living, dancing, and dressing. Satoko admitted that she also became silly and confused, like her peers.

When her health improved in 1946, Satoko enrolled in Tokyo's Pharmaceutical College. She loved nature, and whenever she could, she would stroll along the Yokohama Harbor in Tokyo Bay.

One day, she saw two nuns dressed in their religious habits entering a tiny church. Although not Catholics, and acting on impulse, she and her friend followed the nuns into the church. Satoko found herself standing before a statue of the Blessed Mother, whose beautiful face touched her heart.

The memory of her experience prompted her to learn more about the statue and the nuns. She learned that they belonged to the religious order known as Mercedarians. Although the nuns had been interned during the war and had endured harsh treatment, they were friendly toward the Japanese people, which impressed Satoko and all those who came in contact with them.

Although she came from a strict Buddhist family, Satoko persuaded her father to enroll her young sister in the Mercedarian school. When Satoko visited her sister, she met Mother Angela, who asked her if she had been baptized. With only a little persuasion, Satoko studied for her reception into the Church and was baptized October 30, 1949, taking the name Elizabeth. A few days later she was confirmed and chose the name Maria in honor of the Blessed Mother.

Mother Angela taught her students that if they followed Christ, they might encounter suffering and perhaps even death. This holy nun was a great influence to Satoko, as was Br. Zeno Zebrowski, O.F.M. Conv., who had established a friary in the hills above Nagasaki, the Catholic center of Japan. Each day he would walk from the friary to the town square, where he would beg for Nagasaki's poor. After his day of begging, he would visit the poor of the city to distribute all he had received. Satoko met Br. Zeno shortly after her conversion to Catholicism.

Following the war, the homeless, beggars, criminals, prostitutes, drug dealers, and drifters swarmed into Tokyo and squatted illegally in a shanty village called Ant Town.

The area was designated "ant" because the many people who settled there were as plentiful and as unrecognizable as a community of ants. Because the city fathers viewed Ant Town as an eyesore and a constant reminder of the consequences of military defeat, they frequently and unsuccessfully attempted to destroy it.

Although the residents of Ant Town were those who had lost everything, including their social standing, they were a proud people, opposing crime and any form of charity. Instead, they earned their living by banding together in a community effort to collect junk from refuse heaps, alleys, dumpsters, and even garbage pails, scrounging for anything that could be repaired and sold in the marketplace.

When a picture of Br. Zeno praying the Rosary in Ant Town appeared in the local paper, Satoko was so impressed she visited him in December 1950. He took her on a tour, showing her the homeless, the poor, the vagrants, and the war orphans, who slept on the sidewalks and in areas strewn with debris. Others clustered around campfires or slept in ramshackle huts of cardboard and tin.

That night Satoko could not sleep, thinking of her luxurious surroundings and what the poor had to endure. At twenty-one years of age, she resolved to serve the poor.

A few days after leading Satoko through Ant Town, Br. Zeno asked her to organize a Christmas celebration for the residents. Satoko mobilized the children, taught them songs, and organized the residents into a tableau of the Christmas scene. With the children singing *Gloria in Excelsis Deo,* TV cameras whirred and newspaper cameras clicked. Afterward, there were refreshments to end a perfect evening.

The two main leaders of the Ant Town community, one of them known as the Professor, and the other a convicted felon named the Boss, at first wondered about Satoko's interest in helping the people. They made it known to this wealthy young lady that they would rather starve than accept charity. "We will live in meanest poverty rather than accept food and shelter we have not earned, and we will not permit crime." While both men viewed her with skepticism, Satoko's simplicity and cheerfulness, as well as her obvious love for the Ant Town children, won their trust and admiration.

One special effort proved her sincerity. She obtained a rag-picker's large wicker basket, and after a day of ragpicking, she sold her collection for a hundred yen. To show his pleasure, the Professor presented her with an Ant Town junk cart for her own use.

As might be expected, those who saw her in the streets with the tools of her trade thought this woman of obvious breeding had gone mad—perhaps as a war casualty. Satoko, however, was undisturbed by their stares and the wagging of their tongues.

Every day after collecting junk, Satoko would instruct the children in basic grammar, singing, music, and dancing. Then, after classes, she supervised the children's afternoon baths. For several hours, she could be seen with a towel in one hand and a bar of soap in the other, making certain the children were thoroughly clean.

In spite of her teaching the children, helping the residents, and rag-picking, the Professor still regarded her as the little rich girl who would soon tire of these menial activities. For one thing, every evening she would return to her beautiful home. When she arrived there in the evenings, her mother took all her clothes, shook out the gnats, and washed everything in boiling water.

Soon, however, Satoko exchanged her silk kimonos for the uniform of the ragpicker: a peak cap, a loose gray shirt, and serge trousers. Her parents, so firmly entrenched in Japanese customs and the courtesies of their society, never interfered or resented that their intelligent, beautiful daughter was breaking all the rules observed by women of her class and station.

Satoko eventually took an apartment in Asakusa, a Tokyo neighborhood near Ant Town. She attended daily Mass at a nearby church and soon was bringing the children and many of their parents to Sunday Mass. Many were converted simply by Satoko's example and charity.

When the Ant Town center was built with supplies gathered from the streets of Tokyo, Sotoko set up study rooms for her teaching assignments. Her days would begin with morning Mass and then hours of ragpicking.

Classes would then take place, followed by other chores among those in need. Eventually, the dampness of Ant Town, plus her many exhausting activities, affected her health. But she continued her work, demonstrating to the people her sincere love for them.

Her efforts attracted newspapers, magazines, TV, and radio broadcasters. Often her picture was in the paper, showing her pushing her junk cart. Eventually, the press referred to her as the Mary of Ant Town.

In Japan, the name Mary could refer only to Mary, the Blessed Mother. The reference to the Virgin Mary seemed appropriate, since Satoko was always seen with a rosary around her belt, or holding it in her hands as she prayed her favorite devotion. Satoko always said the rosary was her most valuable possession, since it bore the blessing of the pope. Satoko became so widely known throughout Japan that she received countless letters appealing for her prayers.

Satoko's health eventually failed. She was forced to remain at home, where the Professor visited her, finding her depressed. She wanted to move to Ant Town and live as the people did.

"I want to share the life of the Ant people. I want to work and suffer with them, to rejoice with them as one of them." She also expressed the desire to die for them.

Because of her frail health, it was decided that she should recuperate in the mountains until her health returned. She remained for almost a year, but when she returned to resume her duties, she found that, in her absence, the Boss had hired a married couple to educate the children and supervise their baths. She was no longer needed, she felt, and she was crushed.

But the Boss helped her to adjust. Much to her pleasure, the Professor and all the elders of the community decided they wanted to accept the God of Satoko as their own. They were all baptized.

Satoko left Ant Town and returned to her home in Suginami. With Mother Angela's approval, Satoko decided to become a Mercedarian sister. But on the morning of her departure for the convent, a high fever changed her plans.

The doctor who came to her bedside called her condition critical and gave instructions that she should return to Ant Town.

"She will probably die here, but if she dies at Ant Town," he said, "she will die happy."

The Boss and the Professor arranged a special room for Satoko in the Ant Town center, where statues decorated her room, and where she received the love of the people. As they expected, her health gradually improved.

Tokyo's authorities had attempted to disband the people of Ant Town on a number of occasions to clear the property for a municipal park. The authorities were trying once again, but this time they offered to sell the Ant Towners another piece of land. When the city fathers summoned the Professor to negotiate the sale, Satoko, who was once again confined to bed—this time with tuberculosis—repeated her desire to offer her life to God for the welfare of the people.

When the Professor left after having visited her, she gave him her rosary to take with him. He also brought with him a copy of a book Satoko had written some four years earlier, titled *The Children of Ant Town*.

At the meeting, the city fathers declared, "We have decided to provide Ant Town with a parcel of land for fifteen million yen, payable in five years." The sum could easily be paid in the time allotted.

The sale was completed, and the town moved and settled on its new land on January 20, 1958. Three days later, on January 23, 1958, Mary of Ant Town went to her eternal reward at the age of twenty-nine, having served the people of Ant Town for seven years. She never saw the new Ant Town, for which she had offered her life.

Satoko is buried in the Tama Cemetery on the outskirts of Tokyo, where her grave is often visited by those who admire all she has done.

The story of Satoko spread from Japan to other countries. Because of the overwhelming interest in her life and virtues, the Order of the Franciscan Conventuals decided to promote her cause for beatification as encouraged by the archbishop of Tokyo. The papers concerning the cause were prepared in 1975 following a preliminary investigation into her heroic virtues. The archbishop of Tokyo, Peter Seiichi Schiroyanagi, then instructed that the decree be introduced to the Congregation for the Causes of Saints, which was done in 1984. The little rich girl, who became poor for the love of God's unfortunates, is now awaiting beatification. †

Servant of God Simona Tronci

1960–1984

College Student

ITALY

Simona Tronci was a beautiful girl and normal in all respects. She laughed easily, enjoyed her friends, played on a volleyball team, went on trips and to parties with friends, and joined a band, in which she sang and played the tambourine. She loved life, but above all she loved God.

This love is documented in her diary, in which she wrote her most intimate prayers to God and the Blessed Virgin. Her diary shows the purity of her life, her love of prayer and the Holy Eucharist, and her determination to accept joyfully the will of God.

She was born in 1960 in Cagliari at a time when Pope St. John XXIII was preparing to open the Second Vatican Council. She was born into a military family, one of six children of Leonardo and Maria Tronci. She began her education at the age of six, proving herself to be intelligent, disciplined, prompt, and an eager student.

When she was almost nine years old, she received her first Holy Communion. From then on, she seemed more serious and intense regarding prayer and religious observances.

During her adolescence, all things religious captured her interest. She frequently attended Mass and received the Holy Eucharist, and she happily participated in religious festivals. Although her family was able to supply her with all that she wanted, she preferred to live simply and modestly.

Her love of the Blessed Virgin was evident in the notations made in her diary. In June 1978 she wrote: "Thank you, Madonna, for protecting me and for helping me to resist sin and to follow the way of the Lord. Thank you for accompanying me, to watch over everything and to provide all that is for my good. Mother, you provide what is necessary, your judgments are correct because they come from God. Help me to recognize my faults and to ask forgiveness of Christ Jesus."

Simona continued steadily on the way of perfection and consulted various priests when she felt the necessity. She joined the *Associazione Primavera R. C. C.*, a group devoted to the Catholic Charismatic Renewal. Its members were concerned with growing in the knowledge of God, in prayer, and in the Christian life. Simona was an enthusiastic and devoted member of the group, which consisted mainly of young people.

Simona continued living the ideals of the group during her college years. At first she enrolled in the department of jurisprudence, hoping, in time, to reform unjust laws. But after a year she lost interest in her studies.

She transferred to the theological department of the College of the Sacred Heart in Cagliari. The faculty seemed perplexed that a girl would be interested in classes that seemed reserved for seminarians. For this reason, the faculty examined her intentions closely and presented many questions to determine her motives and suitability. In fact, three times they questioned her, until finally she was accepted.

Her college days were busy with studies and her participation in charismatic groups. She enjoyed discussing religious topics, but above all she loved to pray with her friends. She attended national gatherings, and with evangelical enthusiasm she participated in all their initiatives.

She was content with her studies and her prayer gatherings until January 1983, when her Calvary began. She was only twenty-three years old when a tumor was discovered in her lungs. From then on, she would make trips from Cagliari to Paris for treatment.

By April of that year she was enduring intense pain. Entries in her diary became more numerous. In February she wrote: "I know, my Lord, that you have not abandoned me in all these months, even if I often find it difficult to feel your presence when the pains are strong. But when they fade away, grace becomes a new force that renews me."

Her friends often visited her and were edified by her joyful acceptance of her condition. They realized that her heroism in suffering was measured by her love, generosity, and gratitude to God.

Her diary is filled with prayers of love for God and her willingness to accept all that the Lord ordained, knowing that it was all for the good of her soul. And since she offered her sufferings for the salvation of others, she was content.

Simona next suffered from persistent coughing and a deep exhaustion. Since the physicians saw in her a determination and strength of mind, they did not hide from her the seriousness of her condition. She willingly accepted their diagnosis as the will of God.

Her friends were constant visitors, but one—Alessandra Angius—was able to stay with her. She reported:

"I have to say that, during the illness, Simona showed a great and lavish faith in Jesus. She faced with patience the long series of examination to which she was frequently subjected. We prayed together very often. . . . Her prayer was not applied to herself, but [it consisted] of praise and the offering of her sufferings for the intercessions of her friends. . . .

"Everytime she was subjected to a painful examination or therapy, she was for me the image of the mute lamb that offers itself for others. After chemotherapy treatments she was severely nauseous, but she never complained. . . . To be next to Simona in her suffering moments made me feel the depth of the presence of God."

Simona returned to Cagliari, having made the trip back and forth to Paris for the fourth time. On May 25, 1983, she underwent a surgical procedure. Alessandra recalled that afterward Simona was required to remain immovable because of all the probes in her body for drainage. The scar on Simona's chest was huge, but it reminded her of the wound of Jesus.

In this terrible condition, Simona still maintained a sense of humor, telling Alessandra: "Didn't Our Lord say that the hairs of one's head are all counted? Since I lost all my hair to chemotherapy, He has nothing to count."

Simona's condition worsened and she often vomited. Her legs soon became paralyzed, but she continued to offer her sufferings to God. She prayed: "Dear Jesus, if my body suffers, You still preserve my soul. Preserve it from evil and invade me with Your spirit of serenity and of peace. And to the Virgin Mother, I entrust myself to your arms."

Simona was now a pitiful sight. She lay paralyzed and immovable in the bed, almost deaf, blind, and desperately thin. There were good days, however, when twice she had the joy of assisting at Mass conducted by Msgr. Giovanni Delogu, rector of the regional seminary, together with a group of the seminarians.

During the evening of April 18, the Wednesday before Easter, Simona experienced a crisis. Her friends were removed from the room to pray, leaving only her parents at her bedside. She died soon afterward. She was not yet twenty-four years old.

On Good Friday, the church was filled with hundreds of people who wanted to pray for Simona. People came from nearby towns, who had known her from different parishes. The faculty of theology and her companions in the various religious groups to which she had belonged were also there. Her old companions from high school and her pupils to whom she taught religion attended. With nine priests in attendance, the gathering was an emotional one.

The funeral service for this pure soul was conducted on Easter Sunday in the cemetery chapel of St. Michael. The marble that marks her wall tomb has a framed picture of Simona, the dates of birth and death, and a small dove representing the Holy Spirit, on whom she relied so heavily during life.

Simona's cause of beatification has begun at the diocesan level, and it is hoped that she will be the first saint of the charismatic renewal of the Catholic Church. †

Blessed Teresa Bracco

1924–1944

Martyr of Purity

ITALY

*A*s World War II ravaged her homeland, Teresa Bracco died
at the tender age of twenty. She had been a simple, devout
girl, born into a family of pious Catholic farmers in the village of
Santa Giulia.

From her earliest years, Teresa had a love of the Eucharist and
a tender devotion to the Blessed Virgin. She received her early instructions and love of the Church by following the example of her
parents, who recited a family Rosary every evening after working
hard all day in the fields.

The training she received from her parents was supplemented by
lessons from a holy parish priest, Fr. Natale Olivieri, who gave her
many religious books to read, but most importantly, inspired her life.

At the age of nine she saw a picture of St. Dominic Savio in a
Salesian bulletin with the caption, "Death rather than sin." She

immediately responded, "That goes for me, too." She cut out the picture, pasted it to a piece of cardboard, and hung it over her bed. It remained there as her favorite object of devotion for the rest of her life.

Her piety and her exemplary conduct at school were commented upon by her teachers, since she was often found in church gazing fixedly on the tabernacle, almost as an ascetic in the presence of the Blessed Sacrament. So determined was she to advance in the love of God, she rose early every morning and walked the long distance to the church to attend Mass and receive Our Lord in the Holy Eucharist.

She spent the rest of the day in hard work and prayer, fingering her rosary whenever she could. She was said to have been "different from the other girls," being very modest in speech and dress.

In the autumn of 1943, World War II reached her little village with an intense guerrilla presence. The surrounding mountains and woods afforded countless hiding places for these guerrillas and draft resisters, but the German troops were determined to find them. A fierce clash occurred on July 24, 1944, between the guerrilla forces and German troops on a nearby road. The next day the German troops returned to collect their dead, but they were bent on other activities as well. They looted nearby houses before they burned them and terrorized the people with threats.

The German troops were especially interested in the village of Santa Giulia, since they thought it was a guerrilla stronghold, even though there were indications the guerillas had moved to other regions.

It was during this time that the soldiers seized three girls. One of them grabbed Teresa, took her to a deserted place in the woods, and attempted to rape her. Teresa somehow escaped and ran from the thicket in the hope of getting help from a nearby family, but the soldier caught her and threw her to the ground.

She resisted so forcefully that he became enraged and began to beat her. He then shot her twice with his revolver, and to further vent his rage, he crushed part of her skull with his boot.

Teresa had fulfilled her intention made when she was nine years old: "Death rather than sin."

This twenty-year-old martyr of the virtue of purity was beatified on May 24, 1998. ✝

Servant of God Teresa Di Janni

c%

1872–1950

Mother of Seven

Italy

We have here an example of a mother who reached the heights of sanctity by her faithfulness to duty and her faith, while engaged in the ordinary events of a simple life. Hers was not an easy one, beginning at the age of thirteen, when she was forced to abandon her education because of the sudden death of her mother. Since her father had to work to support the family, it fell to Teresa to remain at home to maintain a neat house, to cook, wash, and care for the children of the family.

Gradually, as a result of an active prayer life, Teresa felt called to the religious life. At the age of twenty-one, she announced her intentions. Her father, however, disagreed with her plans.

In obedience to him she married a sea captain, Joseph Magliozzi and had fourteen pregnancies. Only seven of her children reached adulthood. The loss of the other seven children deeply grieved her, but she accepted their loss as the will of God.

Just as she did in her youth, as a wife she faithfully attended early Mass and received the Holy Eucharist. Afterward, she returned to her home, where she cared for her children, whom she educated in a praiseworthy manner regarding the teachings of the Church. She was careful to teach them right from wrong, explaining to them the necessity for diligent study and the care of those in need.

Every day, in addition to all her household chores and the care of her children, she found time to help the poor and sick. She also explained the faith to those who were unable to attend church services due to physical disabilities. She was a blessing to all with whom she came in contact.

She drew strength for all these charitable endeavors by her almost constant prayer and meditation on the Word of God and from her adoration before the Blessed Sacrament. Somehow, she was able to maintain all these activities in spite of various physical ailments that caused her a great deal of pain. All this she accepted in a spirit of Christian fortitude.

After forty-five years of marriage, she became a widow and was all alone, her children having left home long before. Then another tragedy struck with the beginning of the war. Since the city of Gaeta was a seaport and subject to bombing, she left there and first went to Pastena, where she stayed with her daughter Maria. She next went to the home of her son Alfred in Rome.

After the war, she returned to Gaeta, only to find her home totally destroyed from the bombardment. She was not only alone, but also homeless and with meager funds. For a time she stayed in a small apartment, but then her son Giacinto welcomed her into his home, where she stayed until her death at the age of seventy-eight.

The Church has noted that Teresa reached a height of extraordinary Christian spirituality, and therefore of true Christian heroism in the ordinary events of a simple life, applying herself to her duties, the care of her children, as well as the care of the sick and poor of her community. There was nothing grand or extraordinary about her long life, but it was one closely connected to the love of her Church, especially her love of God and her fellow man. She was totally successful in living the ordinary life, as did Jesus and Mary at Nazareth.

Teresa has been presented by the Church as a role model for mothers and has been given the title Servant of God. Her cause was introduced in 1982. Those who knew her in life now pray that she will soon be raised to the honors of the altar. †

Servant of God Teresa Ferdinandi

1912–1940

Teacher

ITALY

The family of Marino and Maria Ferrotti must have been extraordinary. It has produced two Servants of God, brother and sister, Mario and Teresa, who excelled in their studies and found sanctification in their respective professions. Mario, whose biography is in the book *Saintly Men of Modern Times*, was an attorney and judge, while Teresa found sanctification in teaching.

Born in Todi, Italy, as one of three children, Teresa benefited from the Catholic example of her parents and was provided with an excellent elementary and secondary education. She was almost always at the top of her class. From 1927 until 1930, she obtained a higher education at Perugia and then enrolled in the university known as the Superior Institute of Teaching in Rome. After four years of assiduous study, she achieved a degree in literature in 1934.

During the last year at the university, she taught in Rome in the elementary school *Fausto Cecconi*, where she stayed the following year as a substitute teacher. She then taught in Todi at a grammar school, where she stayed until her death on February 22, 1940. She died at the age of thirty.

As it was for her brother Mario, her love of the Eucharist and the Madonna was primary in her life. She worked hard at stripping herself of faults and increasing in virtue. When illness came upon her, she totally abandoned herself to the will of God.

Also like her brother, she was active in Catholic organizations that benefited youths. She was president of the Ladies of Charity and was the diocesan president of the Female Youth of Catholic Action, for which she worked with intensity.

In 1979, the bishop of Todi introduced causes for beatification for both Teresa and her brother. One wonders if they will be beatified on the same day as were Jacinta and Francisco Marto, who were also a brother and sister duo. †

Blessed Victoria Diez Bustos de Molina

1903–1936

Teacher

SPAIN

As a beloved teacher, Victoria taught many a valuable lesson. But the greatest of all, and the most inspiring to her students, came moments before her death.

She was the only child of Victoria Bustos de Molina and José Diez Moreno, who was deaf, but who was able to support his family competently in a commercial house in the city. She was born in Seville on November 1, 1903, and she was noted during her childhood for her intelligence and talents, especially her artistic ability in painting. She was friendly and lively, and maintained a deep love of the Church. She was especially devoted to the Holy Eucharist and the sacraments, and she regularly meditated and sacrificed her free time for the work of Catholic Action.

During her early years, she struggled to learn God's will for her. Through the prodding of her parents, she decided upon a teaching career. She enrolled at the *Escuela Normal de Maestras* in Seville and graduated brilliantly in 1923.

She proceeded to higher studies, but was constantly concerned about God's will. She felt called to a religious vocation, but hesitated. Since she was an only child, her parents naturally depended on her, especially her father, who was limited by his handicap.

Her prayers for direction were answered in November 1925, when Victoria attended a lecture entitled *The Pedagogical Character of St. Teresa and Her Works*. It was presented at the *Academia*, a residence for women studying at the Normal School under the auspices of the Teresian Association. Victoria left the lecture convinced of her calling in life. She would join the religious association of laywomen founded by Blessed Pedro Poveda Castroverde, which she did in 1928.

Four years later, on July 9, 1932, she made her final commitment. As a member of this association, she was able, according to the rule, to remain at home to care for her parents. Most members, however, lived together as a group.

Another vocation was realized when she decided to live her Teresian vocation as a public schoolteacher. At this time in Spain's history, there was a concerted effort to de-Christianize Spanish education and culture. Many risks were involved, but she maintained that she was unafraid.

Her first teaching assignment was in Cheles, a small town near the Portuguese border. She taught there for a year before being transferred to Nornachuelos, a small town in Córdoba. Although it was a Catholic town, only a few regularly attended Mass.

As for the classrooms, the local government had prohibited the teaching of the catechism and removed all the crucifixes. Every effort in anticlerical Spain was used to eradicate all traces of religion in the educational system. Victoria refused to cooperate and went contrary to the wishes of the government.

Although she did not particularly care at first for the little village of Hornachuelos, she wholeheartedly embraced it, having prayed: "I have asked the Lord to send me to a place where I would be loved less and known little by the people. And after incessant prayer, I obtained from heaven what I had been asking for." But contrary to her wishes, she became well known and was greatly loved by all.

One incident that demonstrated her courage against local authorities was the celebration of Book Day. The mayor entered Victoria's class, and while he spoke to the girls, she examined one of the pamphlets he intended to distribute. She was horrified by what she saw.

One pamphlet was titled: *God Does Not Exist and Has Never Existed; Why the Bourgeois Believe in God.* When the mayor was about to distribute the pamphlets, Victoria refused to cooperate. The mayor was shocked by her reaction and ordered the pamphlets taken away.

It was not only in the classroom that Victoria decided to help her students. With the permission of Fr. Antonio Molina Ariza, the parish priest, she set about organizing a student Catholic Action group as a means of bringing the Gospel into their lives through their assistance to those in need. She also cooperated with Fr. Molina in the work of evangelization, catechesis, the Eucharistic apostolate and adult education, among other activities.

Additionally, since most of her students were poor, Victoria alleviated their suffering by the practical means of collecting clothing for distribution to those in need. She collected money for medicines and even went so far as to make clothing and overcoats for the girls with donated fabrics.

Victoria's self-sacrifice was interpreted as love, not only for her students, but also for the villagers, who benefited from her charity and concern. One of her students admitted, "I liked her and she liked me, too." Another remarked, "She was exceptional in school. In fact, we all respected her."

Throughout her years in the Teresian Association, she advanced in the spiritual life and her closeness to God. She confessed that the secret of her apostolate was praying before the Blessed Sacrament. "I find there the strength, courage, light and all the love I need to help those entrusted to me on the way of salvation."

Victoria's love of the villagers prompted her to pray, "Ask me the price, ask whatever you want from me in exchange for the salvation of this town . . . even if my blood turns cold." Her prayer was on the verge of being answered when the city of Córdoba became entangled in the Spanish civil war. It soon became apparent that this teacher, who so influenced her students against anticlericals, had to be eliminated.

Civil war entered the little village with gunshots. Fr. Molina emptied the tabernacle and entrusted the sacred Hosts to Victoria and his sisters. That same day, the priest was arrested and the church ransacked and burned.

Victoria was teaching a class in religion to a group of women at eight o'clock in the evening of August 11, when two armed men presented themselves and ordered Victoria to join them. She kissed her mother, waved farewell to her class, and calmly left the room with the men.

At first she was taken to a temporary detention center, where she was the only woman. A number of men were detained elsewhere, including Fr. Molina. The next day, at two o'clock in the morning, Victoria and the men were awakened. The eighteen captives were forced to walk for three hours to their new prison.

Accompanied by forty men with rifles, some of the prisoners fell along the way from fatigue and hunger. Others had to carry them along. It was Victoria who encouraged them, saying at one time, "Take heart! I see the heavens opening. The prize awaits us! Let us go! Forward!" And it was Victoria who placed her arms around some of the men, who cried unashamedly.

When the prisoners finally reached their destination at the abandoned mine shaft of Rincon, they realized it was not a prison that awaited them, but a huge pit that would accept their dead bodies. One by one they stood upon a huge stone above the pit and accepted rifle fire. Victoria watched as the men were shot and then fell into the pit. Her parish priest accepted his fate heroically, and then Victoria's time came.

Her captors stood before her and offered to save her life if she would shout only once, "Long live the republic," or "Long live communism." Victoria knelt on the stone, and with her eyes raised to heaven and her arms opened in the form of a cross she shouted, "Long live Christ the King! Long live the Virgin Mother!"

These were her last words. Gunfire sounded, and the body of the brave schoolteacher fell into the pit with the others. She was thirty-three years old.

Her nine years in the village of Hornachuelos moved the hearts of her students and all who had come into contact with her. Her career had been a success. They knew their faith was strong, and she would continue to encourage them with her heavenly prayers.

Victoria was beatified on October 1, 1993. †

Servant of God Victorina Rivara-Perazzo

1867–1957

Mother of Three

Argentina

$\mathcal{V}$ictorina's virtuous parents, Angel Rivara and Maria de Podesta, emigrated from Genoa, Italy, to Buenos Aires, Argentina. It was there that she was born on April 3, 1867. She was baptized in the Church of Grace and received her first Holy Communion in the Buenos Aires church of Balnavera.

At the knees of her mother, Victorina was taught about the goodness of God and learned her first prayers. Because their parents were mindful of their responsibility to provide a good education for Victorina and her sister and two brothers, they all attended the school conducted by the Daughters of Mary Auxiliatrice, who were members of the Salesian order.

Because of her intimate contact with the nuns, Victorina considered joining them in the religious life. But Divine Providence destined another mission for her, that of being an exemplary wife and mother. Various difficulties prevented her entrance into the convent, so that God's will was accepted and willingly embraced.

When Victorina was nineteen years old, she met the handsome Rafael Perazzo and married him on September 22, 1887, when she was twenty years old. The happy ceremony was conducted by the Salesian priest Fr. Valentin Casini in the church of San Carlos. Six years later their first child, Rafael, was born. Following him was Rodolfo and then Maria Angelica.

A few years after the birth of the children, the family moved to the little town of Curuzu Cuatia, where Rafael had hopes of increasing his income so he could better care for his family. After twenty-six years, the family returned to Buenos Aires with their fortunes increased.

After thirty-eight years of marriage, Rafael died in Buenos Aires, leaving his wife and children with a comfortable inheritance and a pleasant home.

Having been educated by the Salesian nuns, Victorina had a deep affection and devotion for St. John Bosco. Together with her daughter, Maria Angelica, Victorina traveled to Europe in 1934 to attend the canonization of Don Bosco. On their return, they traveled with the holy priest Fr. Don Luis Orione, with whom Victorina developed a reverent friendship. In no time at all Victorina, influenced by this good priest, decided to become a Salesian Cooperator. From then on, she would work with the poor and with children as the saint had done.

Ten years after her European journey, she returned to Curuzu Cuati with her daughter and spent the rest of her life there.

Victorina lived a very simple life as an exemplary wife and mother. She transformed her life of work into a "permanent oration." She maintained a rigorous lifestyle for herself and was generous with others.

She had a true obsession to help her neighbors, mainly the poor and children, in conformity with the charism of St. John Bosco. She lived constantly anchored in God, receiving Him in Holy Communion each morning, and likewise practicing to a heroic degree the theological virtues of faith, hope, and charity.

She was always of a sweet, humble, and delicate disposition, preferring to speak little. Because of the comfortable financial situation left her by her husband, she could have lived a life of wealth, vanity, and ostentation, but she avoided these, preferring instead to live simply and to spend her inheritance on the poor.

Due to her interest in Catholic education, she established in Curuzu Cuatia a school named for her husband, San Rafael, which was for the education of men. This she gave to the Salesian Society. Another school, for the education of children, was entrusted to the Institute of the Children of Mary Auxiliatrice. Next to the school, San Rafael, Victorina built the church of San Juan Bosco.

Victorina died a very holy death in Curuzu Cuatia on September 24, 1957, at the age of ninety. She rests today in San Juan Bosco Church in Curuzu Cuatia.

The last action taken on her cause was in 1957. Victorina Rivara-Perazzo awaits beatification. †

Venerable Virginia Blanco

1916–1990

Teacher and Servant of the Poor and Uneducated

Bolivia

*V*irginia Blanco was the second of four children born into a longstanding Catholic family that had gifted Bolivia with distinguished politicians and men of letters, such as Carlos Blanco Galindo, president of the republic. The daughter of Don Luis Blanco Unzueta and Doña Daria Tardio Quiroga of Cochabamba, Bolivia, she was born on April 16, 1916, in the same city in which she died on July 23, 1990.

Hers was a gentle nature. She was always calm and simple and never raised her voice. Her face reflected peace and kindness, which affected all she met. She studied in the recently established College of the Handmaids of the Sacred Heart, where she graduated on the high school level, receiving the Best Student Award in the class of 1933. She was a member of the Sodality of the Daughters of Mary, from which she received a great appreciation of the Eucharist and a deep love of the Blessed Mother.

At an early age she professed an interest in helping others. She became a catechist, preparing children and young people for the reception of the sacraments, a work she continued throughout her lifetime. On more than one occasion, she found it necessary to baptize children in danger of death. And with the *Hermanas Misioneras Cruzadas de la Iglesia*, she organized annual missions of a week's length on the families' properties for the spiritual assistance of the poor workers of Cochabamba.

She displayed a remarkable intelligence. Always eager to increase her knowledge of all that pertained to her religion, she studied at the *Normal Santa Teresa* and at the *Normal Superior de Religion*, where she received her degree when she was thirty-two years old. She served as professor of religion in several public schools for thirty-four years until 1977. At nearly the same time, the education committee of the Episcopal Conference of Bolivia, recognizing her talents, named her coordinating director for the formation of teachers of religion in the Department of Cochabamba, a position she held from 1976 to 1980.

In 1976 her interest in charitable endeavors led her, with the assistance of her spiritual director, Fr. Javier Segura, S.J., to found the Economic Kitchen, which became the Social Service Dining Room, thanks to the support of other distinguished women of the city. This organization continues today to accommodate nearly two hundred mealtime guests daily. During this time she started a soup kitchen in her own home, and in 1976 she opened *El Rosario,* a primary medical clinic for the poor who could not afford other medical facilities.

In addition to all her labors, she spent a great deal of time seeking donations to maintain these charities.

Virginia also opened the *Arte Sacro,* a shop dedicated to the sale of liturgical objects and religious books, whose profits were donated to the Jesuit novitiate.

She was a member of Catholic Action and founded the Woman's Youth Action. Later she became a member of the Woman's Association of Bolivian Catholic Action. She also served as president of the diocesan council and met regularly with parish council presidents. In addition, she founded a number of prayer and apostolic groups and faithfully fulfilled all her responsibilities until her death.

Virginia was distinguished for her deep humility, her charity toward the poor, and her apostolic interests. From friends who knew her well, we learn that she took private vows of poverty and chastity. Although she belonged to a wealthy family, she lived simply and dressed simply, always being neat and modest. Her deep spirituality was reflected in her affection for everyone, regardless of social standing.

Although busy with all her activities, she maintained a deep spiritual life. She focused her life on the Eucharist and Mass, which she attended every day, often a number of times a day. She also spent long hours in prayer in the chapel of her home and always sought the spiritual direction of wise and holy priests.

Additionally, she regularly gathered the poor in her own home for the recitation of the Rosary. She was the inspiration for an organization known as Friends of Bolivia, which was founded by Luisa Lopez and Fr. John J. McCabe after receiving a letter from Virginia Blanco. One of the organizations, supported by The Friends of Bolivia, is known as *Policlinico Rosario*, which was founded by Virginia.

The Society of Jesus in Bolivia recognized Virginia as an outstanding benefactor, while the municipality of Cochabamba awarded her the title of outstanding citizen for her contributions to the material and spiritual development of the city.

Yet another honor was bestowed on her, this one by the bishop of Cochabamba, Armando Gutierrez Granier. She received the *Pro Ecclesia et Pontifice Cross*, awarded by Pope Paul VI "in recognition of her merits as the first president of the Woman's Youth

Action and as a devoted apostle of Woman's Catholic Action, for her untiring collaboration in Catholic education as a professor of religion, and for her loyal cooperation with the bishop at every available opportunity."

Then, in 1988, her loyalty to the Church and the pope was recognized with the honor of receiving Holy Communion from the hands of Pope St. John Paul II on his visit to Cochabama.

After a lifetime of delicate health and having spent so many years in the service of the poor, Virginia died quietly and peacefully during the night of July 23, 1990, from cardiac difficulties. Earlier, she had been administered the Sacrament of the Anointing of the Sick and was given the apostolic blessing of the Holy Father. Her last words were "May Our Lord help me." Her death had an impact on many people at all social levels, who attended the funeral services.

During prayers offered for Virginia at her funeral, the word "saint" was whispered frequently. The mourners reflected on her devotion to the poor, to whom she gave material help, "making available to them whatever she had, her house, its goods and mainly herself."

In the year 2000, the archbishop of Cochabamba, Tito Solari, opened the process of beatification. Testimony of Virginia Blanco's heroic life and virtues has been collected, and a number of commemorative ceremonies have been celebrated in her honor in both Cochabamba and in Rome.

The Delegate Judge for the Process of Beatification, Fr. Miguel Manzanera, S.J., wrote: "Since she will be the first Bolivian laywoman raised to this honor, her beatification will be, without doubt, an event of great significance for the Church in Bolivia." She was declared Venerable on January 22, 2015. †

Wiera (Ida) Francia

1898–1928

Teacher

ITALY

Wiera Francia would be a good role model for those who recognize their own faults, limitations, and difficulties in doing God's will, and strive to overcome nature and reach a deep spirituality, yet still have great difficulty in doing so. She, too, had the same difficulties and had to struggle in the same way. But she did so in such an extraordinary manner that she has been considered for the honors of the altar.

Wiera Francia was not a sunny, playful, outgoing child. Probably because of chronic sickness, she was quiet and pious, but when she was a little older, she admitted to having many faults: She was not as pleasant as she should have been with members of her family; she used hard and brusque words; and she was not above correcting her older sisters.

239

She was somewhat headstrong, too, preferring to do things her own way rather than as her parents wanted. No one would have suspected that from childhood, she would struggle so valiantly against what she called her limitations and faults with such heroic efforts that she would be remembered for her virtues and promoted as one worthy to be imitated.

She had three sisters and a brother, all who lived with their parents and paternal grandparents under the same roof. She loved them dearly and missed them dreadfully later in life, when she had to move to various places outside her native Forli.

She was taught by the Sisters of St. Dorothy in elementary school, but for high school she attended public school, where she excelled in her studies. After graduation, she was destined to work in her father's store, but her teachers persuaded her father to allow her to pursue higher studies based on her excellent marks. He agreed when Wiera won a number of scholarships.

After graduation when she was eighteen, she left home for a university in Bologna. Leaving her family environment was difficult for her. She felt out of place at the university boarding house and had some difficulty making friends because of her quiet demeanor. But she was always ready to help students who were having difficulty with their studies.

She continued her religious practices but was touched by a streak of melancholy, for which she found comfort in religion. It was quite a struggle, however, as she noted in her diary: "Above all, I'm so cold in religious matters, so unmortified, so impatient! Today I would have preferred not to go to church because it bores me to go, and to remain there annoys me. How horrible I am . . . cold, cold, evil."

As Fr. Redemptus M. Valabek, O.Carm., wrote in his *Profiles in Holiness II*, she eloquently exhibited that real virtue was not a natural propensity, but a challenge met and conquered:

"Wiera is a realist. She details her failings: She is too critical, she uses improper language, she is envious, easily discouraged, irascible to the point of crying out of anger without knowing why, she is proud with a subtle pride which hankers after praise even while refusing it, which refuses to bend down and ask for help, which looks down on the person who doesn't care for her, all the while giving the impression of humility. Wiera is ruthless in her self-analysis because she knows that this is how the Lord sees her."

Before she finished her studies she was already teaching. She received her degree in 1920 and a doctorate the following year, but she still felt inadequate and had to force herself to teach. It was probably more of a duty than a love of her calling, perhaps because of her retiring nature.

She began teaching in private schools, and in 1925 she participated in two national placement examinations and won a post teaching mathematics and physics in Lecce. It was here that she met and was guided by a gifted spiritual director.

She stayed only one year in Lecce, then obtained a teaching post in Macerata, which was closer to home. Although fellow teachers and students appreciated her, she was anxious about her work, never satisfied that she was fulfilling her duties completely. Exam time was particularly tormenting to her, since she wanted to give each student a just and fair evaluation, but this seemed a difficult thing to do, considering that she had more than three hundred students.

She suffered when the students did not seem interested, and there were times she had difficulty with discipline. She told of her emotions in her diary and mentioned how she tried to spiritualize her difficulties by remembering the trials Our Lord endured during His lifetime on earth.

In addition to her teaching assignments, Wiera was active with Catholic Action, which she had joined during her teens. Because of her quiet disposition, she was not enthusiastic about the activities on the social scene, but she eventually accepted the demanding position of president of the diocesan section of the organization. She did so only out of a sense of duty, since she "had accepted to work in Catholic Action with extreme repugnance, out of a sense of duty and mortification, because external activity did not attract her. She would have preferred to pray much and also . . . to dream."

But she decided to do as much good as she could for as many people as she could. When she was twenty-five, she passed from the youth organization to the Union of Catholic Women, for which she became regional delegate and then diocesan president. She gave conferences, prepared outlines to be followed, encouraged, inspired, and exhorted, reminding the members that "we have no right to neglect a single person regardless of how distasteful to us contact with him might be. Jesus loves him and died for him . . . in any circumstance look at Jesus, see how He acted."

At this time Wiera listed some of her faults. She claimed to be "bitter, oversensitive, intolerant, harsh, moody, impatient, bad-humored, self-centered." The list went on and on, but she was always striving to overcome these faults, and the interior struggle lasted the whole of her life.

She once declared, "I should conquer myself. I wish I could, but I do not always succeed. I suffer a lot because of it." However, she prayed fervently and continued to strive toward her goal.

During her early years in Forli, she had been influenced by the Carmelites and was now a Carmelite tertiary. Their rule gave her the needed order and organization that appealed to a teacher of math. According to the rule, she first began to pray the Little Office of Our Lady every day and then substituted the whole Divine Office, the official prayer of the Church.

She wore the scapular, or the "little habit," which she called a gift of Our Lady, "a privileged vestment of honor, the emblem of her brotherhood and promise of her motherly predilection, a shield of defense in dangers, a guarantee of peace with God and a foreshadowing of eternal predestination."

In addition to teaching and her activities with Catholic Action, she was faithful to her duties as a tertiary. She attended Mass each morning, received the Eucharist, recited the Office, meditated, read spiritual books, visited the Blessed Sacrament, examined her conscience, recited the Rosary, and when possible, attended Benediction services. Her meditations usually lasted two hours, and her thanksgivings after Communion were, according to her spiritual director, "protracted with her head in hands. . . . She was oblivious to all else around her."

Wiera once wrote, "You've not prayed well if it makes no difference in the way you treat others, in the way you act out your Christian commitment. Authentic prayer necessarily makes a person abound in good works." Wiera prayed well and worked well, never depriving others of the care, advice, or help she could give them, even though her health was almost always precarious.

Although she had several opportunities, Wiera never married. She thought of a religious vocation, but she knew the cloistered life was not for her. She was inspired during Mass to make a private vow of perpetual virginity, which she made October 3, 1926, just two years before her death.

She regarded this act, made after receiving Holy Communion, as her nuptials, and from then on she regarded herself as a "Spouse of Christ." Thereafter, she felt obliged to follow her beloved wherever He went and to do whatever He asked of her.

Wiera had always suffered from poor health. Not helping the matter were her constant struggles at self-control and the overcoming of her faults, the need to be of help to others, and the fulfillment of her difficult duties in life. Wiera soon began to experience physical exhaustion and bouts of amnesia. The doctors ordered complete rest during the summer months, but when she returned to school in the fall, she felt overly burdened with her many responsibilities.

Finally, her condition began to deteriorate to such an extent that, in March of 1928, the doctors wanted to operate. Refusing anesthesia, Wiera offered her ordeal for the intentions of saving souls, for priests, and for the members of Catholic Action. Following a period of recuperation, and in spite of weakness, she returned to school, but during a meeting of Catholic Action she left quickly.

Doctors soon recognized her serious condition and performed procedures to alleviate her sufferings, but when her intestine was perforated, everyone accepted this as an indication of the end.

Wiera was greatly consoled after receiving the Sacrament of the Anointing of the Sick and the reception of the Holy Eucharist. She kept telling family and friends not to cry, that she was in the Lord's good hands, into which she had placed herself years earlier. She received a visit from the local bishop, who gave her a special blessing from the Holy Father. She died on May 28, 1928, at the age of thirty.

In the last entry of her diary, Wiera gives us considerations by which she lived and by which she merited a high degree of sanctity:

"Your sanctification is the first activity to which Jesus wishes you to apply yourself, and He makes you understand this particularly by calling you to the apostolate. But it is not activity made up of solemn and grandiose acts. Holiness is not heroism for a moment, nor even a series of properly so-called heroic acts. Holiness must include one's whole—life is made up of days and instants. Thus, every day, or rather every instant, should contribute to form the building of your holiness. If you wish to become holy, you must not think of beginning next month, or tomorrow or even in an hour. You must begin this very instant. Only if you divide up your activities in this way—hour by hour, minute by minute—will you be able to apply yourself with effectiveness, because it is just in this way that Jesus gives you His grace. Think of being a saint today and begin this very hour, or rather this minute, and afterward let Jesus act." †

Wilhelmina Ronconi

1864–1936

Writer, Poet

ITALY

Can a person who spent a lifetime actively involved in the social problems of her country, one who was an orator on a wide range of educational and cultural subjects, one who introduced a large number of social and religious organizations—could someone like this advance sufficiently in her spiritual growth to be considered for canonization? Such a one could be if she were adamantly attached to the Catholic faith, to the Church, and to the religious and spiritual welfare of the children of God, as was Wilhelmina Ronconi.

Born into a distinguished Italian family of professionals in Pesaro, on the Adriatic coast, Wilhelmina was the sixth child of the family. After a difficult delivery, the mother was in such a weakened state that Wilhelmina was entrusted to a wet nurse, Donna Camilla, who kept the child for three years on a simple country farm.

When Wilhelmina returned to her family home, her older sister Ginevra was obliged to teach her proper manners, which were in keeping with the well-mannered society to which her family belonged. Wilhelmina felt more comfortable in the company of the household servants, and it was two of them, Blaise and Catherine, together with her Aunt Angelica, who took Wilhelmina to church and gave her her first religious training.

The Venerini Sisters provided the rest of her early education, and it was to them that Wilhelmina, or Mina, remained grateful all her life, since it was they who confirmed her in her solid religious education. During her school years, Mina felt the loss of her sisters, who one by one married and left home. At the age of twelve, Mina lost both her parents and was left alone in the family home. Assigned a guardian, she was sent to the best schools in Pesaro, where her personality developed and where she became an admired and accomplished student.

In time her brother-in-law, the mayor of Pesaro, sent her to Rome for higher studies. In Rome she had the good fortune of being educated by some of the best lecturers of the time. She was a brilliant student and was rewarded in 1888 with a doctorate.

When her family fortune was practically exhausted, she hid her difficulties from her highly positioned married sisters and applied for work as a teacher. Assigned to Vercelli in the north, she became an excellent teacher despite the cold climate that adversely affected her. In addition to teaching, she contributed articles to various publications and wrote poetry that was much appreciated.

As an attractive young lady, Mina had several marriage proposals. But she declined them all, deciding instead upon a celibate way of life. This was probably due to her involvement in a number of social issues.

She eventually obtained a teaching transfer to Florence, where she substituted for the director of a school. When a blind youngster expressed a desire to enroll in the school, Mina accepted him and began a lifelong interest in helping the blind. The book she wrote on this subject was in print for many years thereafter.

A transfer to Rome took place two years later, and with the change to a milder climate her health improved. When she was assigned to the Vittorio Colonna School near the Basilica of St. Mary of the Angels, her unique qualities as an educator impressed her students, so that one of them characterized her as "a mother, a nun, an apostle."

Her talents became so widely known that she was called upon to collaborate and give guidance to various associations. She became national secretary of the Society of Blind People and was the first woman to give free lessons at the Soldiers' Home. She was named acting president of the General Workers' Society, whose honorary president was the queen of Italy.

Mina then became active in many other organizations, including the Archaeological Society and the Union of History and Art. Her conferences for these and other organizations were said to have been spellbinding, well-prepared, yet practical. She was also called upon to be part of the National Council of Italian Women, which was involved with the social and moral sector.

The greater part of her energies were spent in her own organization, the Movement for the Moral Life, which busied itself with people of every social standing, especially with slum dwellers. Poor women suffering from ignorance and social injustice tugged at her heart, so she began an educational effort in favor of the poorer classes, with the hope of raising their social standing. Mina helped these women by giving advice, instructing them on the upbringing of children and housekeeping, filling out forms, and teaching the women that they were the heart of the family, and as such were to be respected by the family.

Mina also joined Catholic Action, for which she gave lectures. After one of her conferences, some of the grateful women asked why she didn't preach in church. A youngster said after one of her lectures, "I thought I was in church, and when I came out I made the Sign of the Cross."

She represented Italy in various international congresses and was active in the International Congress on Bad Language, Blasphemy, and Pornography. She also participated in the International Congress on Blindness, the Congress of Popular Libraries, and the National Congress of Italian Women.

She was invited to apply her talents to the prison apostolate and did so with great energy in securing better conditions for both men and women as they progressed through the judiciary and penal systems. She became the most popular figure on the prison scene, giving talks that were practical and helpful. Mina not only gave talks but engaged in other activities, such as bringing newspapers, books, and candy to the women prisoners, writing letters for them, and seeing to the completion of various tasks.

She was startled to learn that women prisoners with young babies or children had to sleep on the same pallet and that some children were left unattended while the mothers worked in the prison. Mina appealed to the queen for help and received cribs and other articles to help to alleviate the situation.

Overwhelmed by the apathetic, ill-kept prisoners, Mina was sympathetic to their misery and did all she could to reform conditions. But the Fascists, unconcerned with reform, finally forbade her to visit the prison. She could do no more, except that she instructed her godchild, Lina Pennisi, to use whatever money remained in her account after her death to establish a home for women released from prison. Such a home was established, according to Mina's wishes.

The Italian government, appreciative of her work, dispensed her from teaching so that all her time could be devoted to her many projects. In 1912, she was appointed to the committee that supervised Rome's reform schools for minors. She quickly realized that the students lacked the loving attention of a mother's concern and created Maternal Action, a group of women who would assist, morally and lovingly, the minors who lived in corrective institutions.

When Arezzano experienced a devastating earthquake, Wilhelmina did all she could to alleviate human suffering. She helped the Red Cross in assisting the wounded and organizing both material and moral aid to those who survived. She was again active when World War I started by giving talks that stressed love of one's country.

To help in supporting the war effort, Wilhelmina organized the School of Popular Eloquence, in which others were educated in various subjects and in public speaking. One of her students was a girl, Lina Pennesi, the daughter of a professor who had never introduced her to any religion. Lina was attracted to Wilhelmina and her work and was eventually baptized and confirmed, with Wilhelmina as her godmother. After Wilhelmina's death, it was Lina who continued her work.

When the war ended, Wilhelmina increased her activities to include teaching courses in health care in conjunction with the Red Cross. She relied heavily on her experience in having visited many military hospitals and tuberculosis wards. Her concern was extended even to include the needs of rural dwellers. At the request of the Ministry of Agriculture, she applied herself to helping farmworkers who were struggling financially and socially.

When fascism began its system of oppression and the centralization of organizations, it limited Wilhelmina's apostolates. Individual efforts dwindled, along with the work of the Movement for the Moral Life. Even her work among the poor of Rome was limited. She quickly realized that the time she would have spent in her many organizations, now denied her, could be spent in deepening her religious life.

During the whole of her teaching career, and the founding of and working for various social organizations, Wilhelmina relied heavily on her religious faith and the principles instilled in her by her family and the training received by the Venerini Sisters in her earliest years. Now fifty-eight years old, Wilhelmina joined the Franciscan Order as a tertiary and soon became the group leader.

Six years later, in 1928, she obtained a special papal privilege, which enabled her to become a Discalced Carmelite tertiary. She wanted this affiliation because of her deep love for Our Lady, under the title of Our Lady of Mount Carmel. Wilhelmina was careful to observe the rules of both orders and to attend the monthly meetings.

Wilhelmina now engaged in another apostolate, that of writing spiritual books. Her first was dedicated to the heart of Jesus and was published by the Vatican Press. Another interest was having the chapel in St. Peter's reopened, which was dedicated to the good centurion, St. Longinus. Inside the chapel was the spear that opened the wound in Our Lord's heart. She used all her persuasive charms in having this converted Roman soldier named protector of the Italian army.

One of her most beloved devotions was toward the House of Loreto, where she made a number of retreats and received great graces. She was named an honorary Lady of the House of Loreto in 1926. Two years later, she visited the shrines of France and then made a pilgrimage to the Holy Land.

Some years later, Wilhelmina became seriously ill and remained so for several months. Although her physicians thought her condition terminal, she improved and resumed her normal activities. While in Turin, where she was called upon to present a series of conferences on the radio, she again fell ill. She died peacefully after receiving the sacraments and the blessings of the Church she so dearly loved.

Wilhelmina has been called a champion of social justice. †

Index of the Women's Occupations
and Difficulties of Life and Health

Abused wife: Maria Carolina Scampone, Maria Aristea Ceccarelli, Praxedes
Fernandez
Amnesia: Wiera Francia
Amputation of leg: Antonietta Meo
Abortion opponent: Angelina Pirini, Alexia Gonzalez-Barros, Hildegard Burjan
Abortion performed on: Dorothy Day
Abortion rejected: Elisabetta Tasca Serena, Gianna Beretta Molla, Hildegard
Burjan, Maria Corsini Quattrocchi
Anemia: Pauline Marie Jaricot
Apostolate of Prayer: Rosa Giovannetti
Appendicitis: Anfrosina Berardi, Angelina Pirini
Arthritis: Concetta Bertoli
Atheist, former: Dorothy Day
Back problems: Alexia Gonzalez-Barros, Rose Price
Baker: Praxedes Fernandez
Blind: Concetta Bertoli
Blind, worked with: Wilhelmina Ronconi
Bronchial condition: Montserrat Grases
Cancer patient: Alexia Gonzalez-Barros, Antonietta Meo, Chiara Luce
Badano, Elisabeth Leseur, Matilde Salem, Montserrat Grases,
Capuchin tertiary: Carmen Garcia Moyon
Carmelite tertiary, O.Carm.: Angelina Pirini, Amata Cerretelli, Annie
Zelikova, Maria Carolina Scampone, Wiera Francia
Carmelite tertiary, Discalced: Anita Cantieri, Josefa Naval Girbes, Wilhelmina
Ronconi
Cashier: Dorothy Day
Catechist: Caroline Kozka, Cleonilde Guerra, Florence Caeros Martinez,
Maria de la Luz Camacho, Maria Corsini Quattrocchi, Praxedes
Fernandez, Rosa Giovannetti, Satoko Kitahara
Catholic Action: Angelina Pirini, Anita Cantieri, Antonia Mesina, Antonietta
Meo, Armida Barelli, Carla Ronci, Cleonilde Guerra, Elisabeth Leseur,

Gianna Beretta Molla, Josephina Vilaseca, Maria Chiara Magro, Maria
Corsini Quattrocchi, Paula Renata Carboni, Pierina Morosini, Rosa
Giovannetti, Teresa Ferdinandi, Wiera Francia, Wilhelmina Ronconi
Child born outside of marriage: Dorothy Day
Childhood, difficult: Maria Aristea Ceccarelli
Childless: Elisabeth Leseur, Matilde Salem
Children, bereaved of: Maria Carolina Scampone
Choir director: Praxedes Fernandez
Clerk: Dorothy Day
Colitis: Mari Carmen Gonzalez-Valerio
Communist, former: Dorothy Day
Concentration camp inmate: Maria Carolina Scampone
Concert artist: Rosa Giovannetti
Convert: Madeleine Delbrêl, Satoko Kitahara
Convulsions: Pauline Marie Jaricot
Cotton mill worker: Pierina Morosini
Cure received: Pauline Marie Jaricot
Dancer: Edel Quinn, Jacinta Marto, Montserrat Grases, Pauline Marie Jaricot
Daughter of Mary: Josephina Vilaseca
Depression, suffered from: Cleonilde Guerra, Wiera Francia
Died in place of daughter-in-law: Marianna Biernacka
Digestive ailments: Paula Renata Carboni
Divorced: Dorothy Day
Dominican tertiary: Praxedes Fernandez
Embroiderer: Crescencia Valla Espi
Embroidery teacher: Josefa Naval Girbes
Epilepsy: Maria Carolina Scampone
Ewing's Sarcoma: Montserrat Grases
Eye problems: Amata Cerretelli, Maria Carolina Scampone, Maria Aristea
Ceccarelli
Eye removed: Maria Aristea Ceccarelli
Faith lost, restored: Dorothy Day, Elisabeth Leseur
False rumors about: Pauline Marie Jaricot
Farm helper: Annie Zelikova, Pierina Morosini
Fevers: Anita Cantieri
Fibroid tumor: Gianna Beretta Molla
Field worker: Concetta Bertoli, Elisabetta Tasca Serena
Focolare member: Chiara Luce Badano, Santa Scorese
Founder of lay association: Amata Cerretelli, Armida Barelli, Dorothy Day,
Fiorella Bianchi, Madeleine Delbrêl, Maria Gioia, Marica Stankovik,
Matilde Salem, Pauline Marie Jaricot, Wilhelmina Ronconi
Flu: Jacinta Marto

Martyr of purity: Antonia Mesina, Caroline Kozka, Marie Goretti, Santa
   Scorese, Teresa Bracco
Mater Misericordiae Lay Institute: Carla Ronci
Medical doctor: Gianna Beretta Molla
Medical instructor: Josefina Moscardo Montalva
Missions, worked for: Anita Cantieri
Miscarriages: Gianna Beretta Molla
Mourned death of child: Maria Carolina Scampone, Praxedes Fernandez
Musician: Edel Quinn, piano; Gianna Beretta Molla, piano; Maria de la Luz
   Camacho, violin; Montserrat Grases, piano; Rosa Giovannetti, piano
   and cello
Nursing assistant: Maria Corsini Quattrocchi
Opus Dei member: Montserrat Grases, Alexia Gonzalez-Barros (admirer of
   Opus Dei)
Orator: Wilhelmina Ronconi
Paralysis: Armida Barelli, Concetta Bertoli
Parents, unloving, irritable: Maria Aristea Ceccarelli
Pediatrician: Gianna Beretta Molla
Peritonitis: Anita Cantieri
Philanthropist: Matilde Salem
Pleurisy: Edel Quinn
Pneumonia: Cleonilde Guerra
Poet: Madeleine Delbrêl, Wilhelmina Ronconi
Political representative: Hildegard Burjan
Poverty, extreme: Elisabetta Tasca Serena, Maria Carolina Scampone
Pregnancies, difficult: Elisabetta Tasca Serena, Gianna Beretta Molla
Prisoners of war: Maria Carolina Scampone, Marianna Biernacka, Marica
   Stankovik, Wilhelmina Ronconi
Prisoner, civil: Dorothy Day
Professor: Luisa Maria Frias Canizares, Maria Corsini Quattrocchi
Proofreader: Dorothy Day
Publisher: Dorothy Day
Purity, martyr of: See Martyrs of Purity
Ragpicker: Satoko Kitahara
Rape victim: Pierina Morosini
Red Cross worker: Santa ScoreseMaria Corsini Quattrocchi, Wilhelmin
   Ronconi
Religious life entered, left: Anita Cantieri, Carla Ronci, Cleonilde Guerra
Rheumatism: Anita Cantieri
Salesian Cooperator: Matilde Salem, Victorina Rivara-Perazzo
Scabies: Maria Aristea Ceccarelli
Scarlet fever: Mari Carmen Gonzalez-Valerio

Sciatica: Amata Cerretelli
Seamstress: Carla Ronci, Francisca Cuallado Baixauli, Pierina Morosini, Praxedes Fernandez, Rachel (Lina) Noceti
Secretary: Edel Quinn, Fiorella Bianchi
Septic peritonitis: Gianna Beretta Molla
Septicemia: Mari Carmen Gonzalez-Valerio
Servant: Amalia Abad Casasempere, Angela Salawa, Aristea Ceccarelli, Praxedes Fernandez
Shepherdess: Praxedes Fernandez
Sickness, lengthy: Amata Cerretelli, Anita Cantieri, Concetta Bertoli
Son was prisoner: Maria Carolina Scampone
Sores over body: Rosa Giovannetti
Spasms: Pauline Marie Jaricot
Speech problems: Amata Cerretelli, Armida Barelli, Concetta Bertoli, Pauline Marie Jaricot
Sports enthusiast: Montserrat Grases
Stepmother, difficulties with: Rose Prince
Surgeon: Gianna Beretta Molla
Tailor: Rachel (Lina) Noceti
Teacher: Incarnación Gil Valls, Maria Chiara Magro, Paula Renata Carboni, Teresa Ferdinandi, Wiera Francia
Television denied to family: Elisabetta Tasca Serena
Textile worker: Florence Caeros Martinez
Thrombectomy: Mari Carmen Gonzalez-Valerio
Tonsilitis: Amata Cerretelli, Antonietta Meo
Tuberculosis: Amata Cerretelli, Angelina Pirini, Annie Zelikova, Edel Quinn, Maria Gioia, Rose Prince, Satoko Kitahara
Tumor: Amata Cerretelli, Carla Ronci
Typhus patient: Paula Renata Carboni
Walking difficulties: Amata Cerretelli
Widow: Amalia Abad Casasempere, Elisabetta Tasca Serena, Eurosia Fabris Barban, Maria Carolina Scampone, Maria Aristea Ceccarelli, Matilde Salem, Praxedes Fernandez, Sofia Ximenez Ximenez, Tarsila Cordova Belda, Teresa Di Janni, Victorina Rivara-Perazzo
Writer: Madeleine Delbrêl, Maria Corsini Quattrocchi, Marica Stankovik, Wilhelmina Ronconi

Bibliography

Bibliotheca Sanctorum. Citta' Nuova Editrice. Rome, Italy, 1987.

Borriello, L., E. Caruana, E., Del Genio, M.R., Suffi, N. *Dizionario Di Mistica.* Libreria Editrice Vaticana. Rome, Italy, no date.

Brown, Ann. *No Greater Love, Bl. Gianna: Physician, Mother, Martyr.* New Hope Publications. New Hope, Ky., 1999.

Celiberti, Michele. *Non Riusciva ad Esser Triste, profilo biografico di Maria Marchetta.* Editrice S.T.E.S.srl. Potenza.

Colafranceschi, P. Carlo. *Serva Di Dio Maria Aristea Ceccarelli.* Provincia Romana Dei Camilliani. Rome, Italy, 1998.

Coles, Robert. *Dorothy Day: A Radical Devotion.* Addison-Wesley Publishing Company, Inc. Reading, Mass., 1987.

Cortesi, Passionista, P. Fulgenzio. *La Serva di Dio Mamma Elisabetta, Elisabetta Tasca Serena.* Postulazione Generale Missionari Passionisti. Rome, Italy, 1991.

Costa, Pier Domenico. *Nilde, Vita Delia Serva Di Dio, Nilde Guerra.* C.d.C. Editrice. Rome, Italy, 1983.

Cowley, Deborah and George. *One Woman's Journey, a Portrait of Pauline Vanier.* Novalis, St. Paul University. Ottawa, Canada, 1992.

Cruz, Joan Carroll. *Secular Saints.* Tan Books and Publishers. Rockford, Ill., 1989.

Cunningham, Joseph W. *Blessed Gianna Molla.* Immaculata magazine. Libertyville, Ill., July/August, 1998.

Cunningham, Joseph W. *Blessed Gianna Beretta Molla.* Signs and Wonders for Our Times. Fall, 1998.

D'Amando, Filippo. *Una Mistica Motorizzata, Carla Ronci.* Editrice Elle Dl Cl. Turin, Italy, 1989.

D'Amando, Filippo. *The Servant of God Carla Ronci of the Lay Institute Mater Misericordiae.* Eco Editrice. Italy, 1987.

Decretum Lucen. Canonizationis Servae Dei Anitae Cantieri. Rome, Italy, 1991.

Delbrêl, Madeleine. *We, the Ordinary People of the Streets.* William B. Eerdmans Publishing Co. Grand Rapids, Mich., 1966.

DeSahb, Roland. *Mathilde Salem, Alep-Syrie 1904–1961.* Imprime sur les Presses de la Fondation Georges et Mathilde Salem. Alep, Syrie.

Dollen, Fr. Charles. *Charity without Frontiers: The Life-Work of Marie-Pauline Jaricot.* The Liturgical Press. Collegeville, Minn., 1972.

Duff, Frank. *Edel Quinn*. Legion of Mary, De Montfort House. Dublin, Ireland, 1999.

Fernando da Riese Pio X. *For the Love of Life: Gianna Beretta Molla, Doctor and Mother*. 1981.

Fortunato, P. Passionista. *La Beata Antonia Mesina*. Giovane di Azione Cattolica Uccisa per la Sua Purezza. Nettuno, Italy, no date.

Hanley, O.F.M., Boniface. *Ten Christians*. Ave Maria Press. Notre Dame, Ind., 1975.

His Holiness Pope St. John Paul II. Translated by Gerald H. Malsbary, Ph.D. *Beatification Decree of Gianna Beretta Molla, Apostolic Letter*, in which the "Honors of the Blessed" are decreed for the Venerable Servant of God, Gianna Beretta Molla. 1994.

Kaczmarek, Tomasz and Flavio Peloso. *Lights in the Darkness 1939–1945*. Michalineum. Poland.

La Beata Angela Salawa Dell'Ordine Francescano Secolare. Pubblicazioni Agiografiche Francescane. Rome, Italy, 1991.

Lanzoni, Rev. Riccardo. *Nilde Guerra, Scritti*. Tipografia Faentina. Faenza. 1988.

Leseur, Elisabeth. *My Spirit Rejoices: The Diary of a Christian Soul in an Age of Unbelief*. Sophia Institute Press. Manchester, N.H., 1996.

Livi, P. Stanislao. *Mamma Carolina, Il Vangelo della Carita di una Laica*. Convento Cappuccini. Le Celle. Cortona. 1996.

Medeiros, Rev. Humberto S. and Rev. William F. Hill. *Jacinta: The Flower of Fátima*. Catholic Book Publishing Co. New York, N.Y., 1946.

Miller, William D. *Dorothy Day: A Biography*. Harper & Row, Publishers. San Francisco, 1982.

Moynihan, O.P, Anselm. *Edel Quinn*. The Legion of Mary. Dublin, Ireland, no date.

Moynihan, O.P, Anselm. *Edel Quinn: A Life in the Trinity*. Dominican Publications. Dublin, Ireland, 1984.

Olive, O.P, Fr. Martin-Maria. *Praxedes: Wife, Mother, Widow and Lay Dominican*. TAN Books and Publishers, Inc. Rockford, Ill., 1987.

Pacholczyk, Ph.D., Tadeusz. *Struggles with Pregnancy and the Generosity of Blessed Gianna*. The Society of Blessed Gianna Beretta Molla. Philadelphia, Pa., article.

Peffley, Mary. *Woman of Faith: The Life of Edel Quinn*. New Hope Publications. New Hope, Ky., 2000.

Picaro, Carmencita. *Anche sul Mare Volano Le Aquile, biografia della serva di Dio Santa Scorese*. Missionarie dell'Immacolata-Padre Kolbe. SAB, San Lazzaro di Savena. Bologna. 1999.

Pietro Delia Madre Di Dio, O.C.D., P. *Anita Cantieri*. Postulazione Dei Carmelitani Scalzi. Capannori-Lucca, Italy, 1955. Company. Piacenza, Italy, 1986.

Pilloni, Clemente. *Innamoratissima di Gesu, Simona Tronci (1960–1984)*. Curia Provinciale Dei Frati Minori Cappuccini. Editrice Velar s.p.a. Gorle (BG), Italy.

Riabilitare l'Amore, profilo di Adele Bonolis 1909–1980. Book.

Suenens, Leon-Joseph Cardinal. *Edel Quinn: Envoy of the Legion of Mary to Africa*. C.J. Fallon Ltd. Dublin, Ireland, 1962.

Terzi, Ignazio. *Le Due Corone, Verginita e Martirio in Pierina Morosini*. Coordinazione a Cura dell'Opera Barbarigo. Bergamo, Italy, 1984.

Valabek, O.Carm., Fr. Redemptus Maria. *Holiness is Ordinary: Maria Carolina Scampone*. Profiles in Holiness I. Edizioni Carmelitane. Rome, Italy, 1996.

Valabek, O.Carm., Fr. Redemptus Maria. *Wilhelmina Ronconi: Camelite Tertiary*. Profiles in Holiness II. Edizioni Carmelitane. Rome, Italy, 1999.

Valabek, O.Carm., Fr. Redemptus Maria. *Holiness Is a Struggle: The Witness of Wiera Francia, Carmelite Tertiary*. Profiles in Holiness II. Edizioni Carmelitane. Rome, Italy, 1999.

Valabek, O.Carm., Fr. Redemptus Maria. *The Life and Witness of Amata Cerretelli, T.O.Carm.* Profiles in Holiness II. Edizioni Carmelitane. Rome, Italy, 1999.

Vishnewski, Stanley. *Meditations of Dorothy Day*. Newman Press. New York, N.Y., 1970.

Walls, Mother Mary Celestine. *I Knew Edel Quinn*. Legion of Mary, De Montfort House. Dublin, Ireland, 1998.

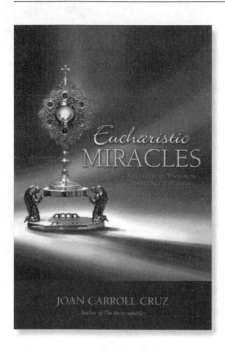
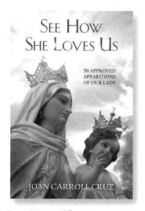
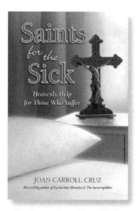

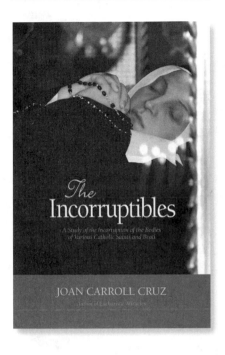
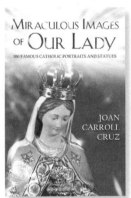
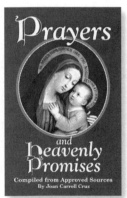

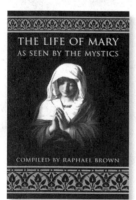
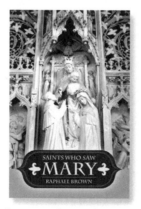
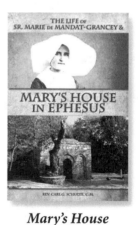

Spread the Faith with . . .

TAN · BOOKS

A Division of Saint Benedict Press, LLC

TAN books are powerful tools for evangelization. They lift the mind to God and change lives. Millions of readers have found in TAN books and booklets an effective way to teach and defend the Faith, soften hearts, and grow in prayer and holiness of life.

Throughout history the faithful have distributed Catholic literature and sacramentals to save souls. St. Francis de Sales passed out his own pamphlets to win back those who had abandoned the Faith. Countless others have distributed the Miraculous Medal to prompt conversions and inspire deeper devotion to God. Our customers use TAN books in that same spirit.

If you have been helped by this or another TAN title, share it with others. Become a TAN Missionary and share our life changing books and booklets with your family, friends and community. We'll help by providing special discounts for books and booklets purchased in quantity for purposes of evangelization. Write or call us for additional details.

TAN Books
Attn: TAN Missionaries Department
PO Box 410487
Charlotte, NC 28241

Toll-free (800) 437-5876
missionaries@TANBooks.com

 TAN·BOOKS

TAN Books is the Publisher You Can Trust With Your Faith.

TAN Books was founded in 1967 to preserve the spiritual, intellectual, and liturgical traditions of the Catholic Church. At a critical moment in history TAN kept alive the great classics of the Faith and drew many to the Church. In 2008 TAN was acquired by Saint Benedict Press. Today TAN continues to teach and defend the Faith to a new generation of readers.

TAN publishes more than 600 booklets, Bibles, and books. Popular subject areas include theology and doctrine, prayer and the supernatural, history, biography, and the lives of the saints. TAN's line of educational and homeschooling resources is featured at TANHomeschool.com.

TAN publishes under several imprints, including TAN, Neumann Press, ACS Books, and the Confraternity of the Precious Blood. Sister imprints include Saint Benedict Press, Catholic Courses, and Catholic Scripture Study International.

For more information about TAN,
or to request a free catalog, visit
TANBooks.com

Or call us toll-free at
(800) 437-5876